SHARING GOD'S LOVE

SHARING GOD'S LOVE

John F. Marshall, O.F.M.

THE LITURGICAL PRESS

Collegeville   Minnesota

To Teresa Ann Popravak

Cover design by Placid Stuckenschneider, O.S.B.

Nihil obstat: Joseph C. Kremer, S.T.D., *Censor deputatus. Imprimatur:* +George H. Speltz, D.D., Bishop of St. Cloud, Minnesota, June 22, 1981.

Library of Congress Cataloging in Publication Data

Marshall, John F., 1922–
    Sharing God's love

    1. Meditations.   I. Title.
BX2182.2.M33   242   81-11794
ISBN 0-8146-1068-4   AACR2

Contents

Foreword

You return from a trip and friends ask how you liked the accommodations—the rooms, the service, the food. Were the people friendly? Were there problems? Was it a vacation to remember? Would you share your experiences?

There are accommodations and experiences of another kind to share—between God and people. But since God is God and people are his creatures, it is not possible for one to substitute absolutely for the other. The two are forever different.

When God created the human race, he accommodated his infinite existence to the product of his love—to the image of himself, us, whom that love brought into existence out of nothing. God did this in such a way that we creatures could actually share his limitless being and, in our flesh-limited ways, could also reflect his infinite being. We do this by sharing our lives in keeping with God's intention when he made us—to share our knowledge, love, and service.

This book is a series of meditations about how God shares our humanity and how we share, or fail to share, God's divinity. In every Mass, as the priest prepares the gifts for the sacrificial meal, he prays: "By the mystery of this water and wine may we come to share in the divinity of Christ, who humbled himself to share in our humanity." These meditations delve into that mystery of sharing. They have taken form out of silent prayer, Scripture, spiritual reading, the insights that friends shared with one another, and the rich testimony of the world. Particular inspiration has come from the central theme of the Franciscan adventure, that is, the incarnation of our Lord Jesus Christ. That mystery of accommodation and sharing was again given flesh in the life of St. Francis of Assisi.

The only way to accomplish fruitful sharing, whether it be God's sharing our humanity or our sharing God's divinity, is through assimilation of one into the other. What a heavenly concession! The means to this sharing is love.

For proof, consider St. Paul's classic commentary on this virtue: "Love is patient and kind; love is not jealous or boastful; it is not arrogant or rude. Love does not insist on its own way; it is not irritable or resentful; it does not rejoice at wrong, but rejoices in the right. Love bears all things, believes all things, hopes all things, endures all things" (1 Cor 13:4-7) Paul is simply saying that love always stands selfless, ready to share.

How can we begin to meet this challenge of sharing? A good question to ask might be: "What shall I render to the Lord for all his bounty to me? I will lift up the cup of salvation and call on the name of the Lord" (Ps 115:12-13). And then what do we do with that cup? As the ancients did to show gratitude, we overturn it to spill its contents, which are our lives. God's divinity and our humanity may then blend into a compatible unity and so bring to happy completion the only intention God had in mind in creating the world.

St. Paul begs us to accept this sharing. He told the Philippians:

> So if there is any encouragement in Christ, any incentive of love, any participation in the Spirit, any affection and sympathy, complete my joy by being of the same mind, having the same love, being in full accord and of one mind. Do nothing from selfishness or conceit, but in humility count others better than yourselves. Let each of you look not only to his own interests, but also to the interests of others. Have this mind among yourselves, which was in Christ Jesus (2:1-5).

St. John comments also on that attitude of Christ: "Beloved, if God so loved us, we also ought to love one another" (1, 4:11).

God on Mount Horeb called on Moses, who answered, "Here I am." God continued, "Do not come near; put off your shoes from your feet, for the place on which you are standing is holy ground" (Exod 3:4-5). The ground we stand on is no less holy than Horeb's. Indeed, since God the Father loved us so much as to send his own Son and since the earth has been drenched with the blood of the same Son, it is the more holy. God sent his Son to share our world that we might better share it with others. In this mystery, we can all participate.

No priest celebrates the Sacred Mysteries without wishing he might have shared more generously and sacrificially the very life of the risen Lord through more faith in and love for Jesus. John the Baptist confessed that he was not worthy to share the life of the Lamb of God. Whatever the sentiments of the Baptist, Jesus made us worthy to share the very life of God. In fact, he commanded it! "Love one another. Such as my love has been for you, so must your love be for each other" (John 13:34). The gift we share we must share with others. Sharers in the mystery of God on earth, we will come to share fully the majesty of God in heaven.

Acknowledgements

It doesn't take much courage to write a book that is self-serving. The market endures a glut of books with the prime purpose of selling an author or bargaining for approval from a gullible public. Such books, more compulsive than creative, cater to idle curiosity. They may arouse or incite, but they seldom inspire.

To plan a book that proposes ultimate destinies, first causes, and lasting goals, on the other hand, calls for considerable courage — and encouragement. If the author of such a book is to do justice to his scriptural attempt to write about God as merciful, provident, and loving, he must himself be sincerely of God, thankful for him, and prayerfully in love with him.

More as a matter of faith-admission than a statement of fact, it took courage to write this book. It also took encouragement. I received the encouragement from many wholesome people and the courage from the Holy Spirit.

For the encouragement I am especially grateful to James C. G. Conniff, editor and agent, who unsparingly barraged me with sound criticism, healthy suggestions, and stylistic recommendations, always with a saving sense of humor. Without his professional guidance and direction, I doubt that you would enjoy the pages which follow.

I am especially grateful, also, to my fellow friars — Fr. Roy M. Gasnick, O.F.M., and Fr. Cassian A. Miles, O.F.M., respectively the director and assistant director of communications for Holy Name Province of the Order of Friars Minor — for the unstinting support and encouragement which they have afforded me during the long ordeal of writing and rewriting.

To Mary McGavisk, who typed the initial and final manuscripts, mere acknowledgement is not enough. Her enduring patience and plain hard work became, for me, one of the inspirational by-products of this book. With prayer alone can I fully repay her.

In that same spirit of prayer, I invite you to read on. Courage!

JOHN F. MARSHALL, O.F.M.

May 5, 1981

11

1

Jesus Treats Us as Persons

One of the acute pains of experience comes when people misread our intentions, mistake our goodwill, doubt the wisdom of our decisions. That's when the last and only appeal is to God himself. God always understands.

One day the disciples of John the Baptist approached Jesus and asked him, "Are you he who is to come, or shall we look for another?" (Luke 7:20). Our Lord turned to the crowd and protested:

> "To what then shall I compare the men of this generation, and what are they like? . . . For John the Baptist has come eating no bread and drinking no wine; and you say, 'He has a demon.' The Son of Man has come eating and drinking; and you say, 'Behold a glutton and a drunkard, a friend of tax collectors and sinners!' Yet wisdom is justified by all her children" (Luke 7:31, 33–35).

More than once Jesus sighed because people persisted in misunderstanding him. To the woman at the well, "If you knew the gift of God, and who it is that is saying to you, 'Give me a drink,' you would have asked him and he would have given you living water" (John 4:10). To a gathering at the Temple, "Why do you not understand what I say? It is because you cannot bear to hear my word" (John 8:43). To the disciples en route to Emmaus, "O foolish men, and slow of heart to believe all that the prophets have spoken!" (Luke 24:25). To the Apostle Philip, "Have I been with you so long, and yet you do not know me, Philip?" (John 14:9). When Jesus says, "Learn from me, for I am gentle and lowly in heart" . . . (Matt 11:29), he invites us to look directly into his heart — a heart so widely misread, so often misunderstood.

Although the ways of God are not always those of the world, it was along the byways of the world that Jesus walked. Jesus spoke often in parables but with an other-worldly wisdom. He waited patiently for men and women to hear and understand him. Whether he taught the lesson of the lost sheep, the misplaced coin, or the prodigal son, he invited each of us to look into the infinite depths of his humble heart.

Jesus knew that each person had unique problems and a particular need for him. Whether it was Magdalene, Zacchaeus, Peter, or Judas, Jesus adapted to the individual. He never classified people. He never grappled with crime problems, juvenile crises, or race issues. Even when he berated the Pharisees, the individual was never lost in the crowd. It was always the person — two grief-laden sisters, an innocent child, a publican, a thief, a police captain, a prostitute. Yet, it was in dealing with the individual with all his heart that he, our Lord and God, was most misunderstood.

Too often nobody misses one lost sheep out of a hundred. It is easy to write off a lost coin. A wayward son deserves to sleep in the bed which he has feathered. Better for Mary to sell the precious perfume than to wash the feet of Jesus; the money can be used for the poor. How does Jesus understand it? "She has done a beautiful thing to me. . . . You always have the poor with you, but you will not always have me" (Matt 26:10-11). Jesus is really saying that he is one of the poor. In a different manner he is still with us, still poor, still waiting for us to want to learn about him.

A movie on basketball is entitled *One on One*. A television commercial in boasting about the millions of burgers sold reminds us that they were cooked "one at a time." At the Olympic games in Montreal, sportscasters wove into their radio and television coverage "up close and personal" background stories of athletes. The heart of Jesus accommodates itself to each of us. How personal can a person get? One-on-one mercy, understanding, encouragement — that is Jesus. He says to us, one at a time, what he said to the blind Bartimaeus at Jericho, "What do you want me to do for you?" (Mark 10:51). Jesus calls us friends. Friends easily adjust to one another. Friends share. Friends are up close and personal.

The Cross means sacrifice, dedication, humiliation, love. Jesus adjusts himself to the Cross first by carrying it and then by letting himself be nailed to it. This is his way of adjusting to us. This is his way of love. There is no better way to share with others than by helping them carry their crosses while taking a firmer grip on our own. There is no better way to love.

Jesus had no adjustment problem when it came to speaking. He spoke with authority. In the synagogue at Nazareth, his audience marvelled at his discourse. On Mount Tabor his Father's voice from a bright cloud testified to his speech: "This is my beloved Son with whom I am well pleased; listen to him" (Matt 17:5). Jesus was the only person on earth who ever could say, "I am the way" or "I am the resurrection." Those who have an up-close and personal faith in Jesus do not misread or misunderstand his pronouncements. They, too, have a passion for the individual.

Accommodation does not come easy when the adjustment is to Jesus. He never said it would. He told us we cannot follow him by leaving our crosses behind. We cannot be like him without looking at our crosses and seeing ourselves upon them. Like friends, our crosses are up-close and personal. At our death we will know that the greatest cross we carried on earth was our greatest friend. Through it we accommodated ourselves to Jesus. For that he will reward us with accommodations in heaven that eyes have not seen nor ears heard.

2

A Lesson in Perseverance

St. Luke's Gospel contains the story of the crafty manager who squandered his wealthy employer's property. Fearing that he would be dismissed, the manager shrewdly set about to save himself from total discredit. Without panic, he called in his master's debtors and reduced their debts. He wanted to ensure his welcome into their homes after his dismissal. Upon learning about this cunning move, the master gave him credit for being so enterprising. Why? Jesus' answer to his disciples, "For the sons of this world are wiser in their own generation than the sons of light" (Luke 16:8), must have confused them, as it does us.

Truly this is a strange story coming from Jesus who usually spoke the plain language of the parable. Surely he cannot be encouraging deceit. What is Jesus telling us? A story with tongue in cheek? A bit of humor? If so, it is very uncharacteristic of anything Jesus ever said. Jesus taught with words carefully chosen to bring the truth to humankind. He was not addicted to the merely entertaining story. In this instance he must have been telling a wisdom story to teach us that even wayward acts can offer some instruction to those who accept his way. A criminal's actions are at times more consistent than the conduct of some Christians. Once a commitment to crime is made, a criminal directs all his or her strength toward it. The game plan must not fail. A criminal suffers adversities to overcome obstacles. An entire life may be spent perfecting crime.

In itself, consistency does not guarantee heaven. But there is some merit to it—consistent conduct is predictable. Compare this quality with the wavering faith of many Christians—now on fire with renewed purpose, now cool to the exercise of faith; now excited in the promises made by Jesus, now excused in the liturgy. They follow Christ, but without follow-through. They say one thing, but do another. Why sing hymns on Sunday if they are out of tune in liv-

16

ing the truth on Monday? The result is neither consistency nor Christ. The only predictable flaw is inconsistency. The predictable cure is the virtue of perseverance. A gift of the Holy Spirit, it is freely given when freely asked for.

Consider David of the Old Testament who indeed was very consistent, first as a sinner, later as a penitent. Once David turned away from sin, he prayed, "Restore to me the joy of thy salvation, and uphold me with a willing spirit" (Ps 51:12). After he had directed himself toward God, whatever the cost, he did not change his pledged word. He anticipated another champion of consistency, St. Paul, who also reformed his ways. Paul wrote:

> And you, who once were estranged and hostile in mind, doing evil deeds, he has now reconciled in his body of flesh by his death, in order to present you holy and blameless and irreproachable before him, provided that you continue in the faith, stable and steadfast, not shifting from the hope of the gospel which you heard . . . (Col 1:21-23).

Where could we find a better exposition of perseverance? We must accommodate ourselves to a once-and-for-all allegiance to Jesus.

We sense an urgency in the follow-up words of Jesus to his disciples. As soon as he got the termination notice, the manager told the debtors, "Sit down quickly" (Luke 16:6). So little time. The notice and reaction were practically simultaneous. There is no tomorrow for the manager. Tomorrow exists for no one, not even God. There is only today and its immediate possibilities. Each day brings a prudent urgency. Every day somewhere someone receives a termination notice. For some it is their last day on earth.

God's ways are obviously not our ways. However, with his help and an assist from the parable of the wily manager, the constancy of the wicked can teach us the merciful consistency of Jesus. The method of the criminal is not totally unlike the manner of Jesus. Both follow through. Hand in hand with Jesus, irrevocably in love with our Master, in step with the Savior, let us leave on earth but one set of footprints.

3

Prayer Problems? A Solution

God is the beginning and end of all prayer because God is love. True love initiates all that is good and brings it to a happy completion. Since God is always listening, the only problem about prayer is the willingness to pray. In a day when we doubt so much that anybody is paying attention or wants to understand, we need to remind ourselves that this is not so with God. When Jesus asked, "What do you want me to do for you?" (Mark 10:51), he cancelled out all excuses for not praying to him and through him.

The Apostles James and John made a farce of prayer when they asked Jesus if they could sit one on his right and the other on his left when he entered his glory. Jesus mildly rebuked them for their short-sighted proposal. Theirs was not so much a prayer as it was a personal, somewhat selfish wish. They had the makings of a real prayer problem. This is a problem most of us face each time we pray.

It was on a dry and dusty day that Jesus happened upon a Samaritan woman drawing water at the village well. To Jesus' request for a drink she responded, "How is it that you, a Jew, ask a drink of me, a woman of Samaria?" (John 4:9). This was all that Jesus needed to hear to enter her searching heart. She had expressed half of a perfect prayer. She had overcome half her problem. Curious but cautious, she tackled the other half — the need to listen. A marginal accommodation was taking place. There was yet much doubt, but there was the continued listening. She had overcome her fear about the asking. Almost unconsciously, she invited that conversation. She was about to make her last and perhaps most difficult adjustment. She found it difficult to listen to Jesus because her life was a shambles, in need of cleansing. Her heart, where God's Word belonged, needed some diligent housecleaning.

Jesus immediately diagnosed her prayer problem as one not of asking but of receiving. He adjusted himself to become the partner in

18

solving this problem of listening. Without carrying the conversation, his speech brought out the best in listening from her. She began to share.

St. Paul's classic description of love is particularly descriptive when referred to God. God is patient love, kind love, never rude love, never self-seeking love. Since God is love he is not prone to anger, does not brood over injuries, does not rejoice in what is wrong, sets no limits to forbearance, never fails (1 Cor 13:4ff.). The problem was not Jesus' but the woman's. Jesus is unalterably disposed toward us. His motive is always love.

Like the Samaritan, we have a peck of problems when it comes to disposition. If we listen to what Jesus speaks, we realize that it is not possible to exploit his love. Christ's love absorbs the attempt itself. In trying this approach we become the more lovable. Being love, God is infinitely adjustable. Since he can only love, what has he to gain or lose? It is we who lose out by turning prayers into wishful thinking and making them real problems.

As with any good examination of conscience, Jesus at the well witnessed the probing of the woman's past. Gently he reminded her that she had too many husbands, a lifestyle hardly conducive to prayer. The garden bed of her life was untidy with weeds.

Almost, as if in passing, like an expected remark of a friend, Jesus said, "Go, call your husband . . . ." (John 4:16). Having had five husbands, the woman must have imagined that the sweet mystery of life would solve itself with each mismarriage. Instead she saw mystery give way to misery. And then, at the well, that misery sat at arm's length from mercy. The process of mutual adjustment was in high gear — not so much asking, but the joy of receiving. She who had five husbands began to accept and experience the happiness of becoming the bride of Christ. She acknowledged her errant ways. Engaged at last in prayer to a singular love, her heart beat with happy anticipation. She spoke less, listened more. In the presence of the Word, prayer words became superfluous. Later, words of praise flowed freely.

Is not this the encouraging model of a reconciliation dialogue among priest, penitent, and God as they share with one another? With more relief than repugnance, the woman exclaimed, "He told me all that I ever did" (John 4:39). And all because Jesus gently helped her to recall her sins, helped her to pray, helped her to share.

Who could ask for more? Love had taken its risk, and she who surrendered to the grace of prayer came off a gracious winner. Little did she suspect that it was a sure bet. It is no contest when Jesus invites us to play for the high stakes of the beatific life. The odds were infinitely in her favor. She placed her life before the one-time stranger who was now her Messiah. In admitting her past grief she found a present joy. She had listened to a good confessor with her heart. Now, instead of counting husbands, she could tally up her blessings. Topping them all was the gift of persevering prayer from a humble and penitent heart.

A hardening of the heart could have triggered very easily a stinging insult against Jesus for his bold words. With quick dispatch and a flurry of her skirt, she could have departed the scene in a huff. She did not. She adjusted. She harrowed her life with humility and raked it with sincerity. Once the ground was broken, it was ready for the seed. She died to Jesus. "But to all who received him, who believed in his name, he gave power to become children of God" (John 1:12). She had solved her problem.

4

God Loves the World

Basic to our faith is the belief in three divine Persons who are one God. The Trinity is the profoundest of all mysteries. Another mystery that flows from the Trinity is the mystery of love. God is that mystery, God is love. Since God is love, he has no choice but to love himself. Even though we do not understand this fully, we do have the revelation of it, the written account of it, the acceptance of it—but above all we have participation in it. We experience somewhat that love with which God loves himself.

St. John tells us that "No man has ever seen God" (1 John 4:12). Yet all around us we can see, just for the looking, God's visible love. Evident signs of God's love abound on all sides—flowers, birds, a smile, a cloud. These are also signs of God's love for himself. How he must have enjoyed himself when he created the world! The Bible tells us how satisfied he was when he looked out over the world his hand had created. He surveyed his work and saw that it was good. His motive for creating a good world had to have been his love for himself.

By definition love has to express itself. Eternally satisfied with one another, the Persons of the Trinity enjoy an infinite mutual love. They are always outdoing each other, but without ever surpassing one another in love. What a happy mystery. In creating the world God also created a need, the need to have some creatures return that love. Since God created this need in himself, no one can deny it in us. Only one thing can fill this need. There must be an emptying of self, whether by God or us. The need to have love come back to us is then satisfied.

The greatest expression of emptying the self are the words of Jesus, "Greater love has no man than this, that a man lay down his life for his friends" (John 15:13). He not only said these words but backed them up with his own death. He died for us on Calvary after

21

first calling us his friends. Since even God can't do more than give his own life, he could not love us more. This act of love should give us some clue to the way God loves himself.

True love offers itself freely and when reciprocated is freely accepted. From man's first day on earth love was at risk. Man could refuse and did. Man could deny and he did just that. This is what makes love most vulnerable. Instead of the joy of being loved now, there can be the sadness of love denied. Instead of the happiness in loving another, there can be the selfish misery of love withheld.

When the notorious Willie Sutton was asked why he robbed banks, he replied with some surprise, "Because that's where the money is." Trumpeter Louis Armstrong, loved around the world, when asked to define jazz, responded, "Lady, if you have to ask, you'll never know." In other words, jazz is all answer. Why do men climb mountains? The peaks are there. Why is a sunset, a waterfall, a song, or a fawn so beautiful? The beauty is there. By being there they make a world beautiful.

Now the key question, Why love God? Because he is love and loves himself in such a way that he created in us the need to love and be loved. Love is the whole answer. If we insist on asking why, we will never know. God's love is an absolute gift, but we will never know that until we accept it. We will then come as close to understanding love as we possibly can. "In this is love, not that we loved God but that he loved us . . ." (1 John 4:10).

One night St. Francis of Assisi with tear-filled eyes spoke the most disheartening words a man could speak, "Love is not loved." When that occurs, life is not lived. When we who need to love and be loved turn our backs on God who is love, who fills these needs, what else could Francis do but weep?

The psychoanalyst Erich Fromm tells us that "Love is the only satisfactory answer to the problem of human existence."[1] What problem? Our only problem is not loving as Jesus loves us. We — not God — create this problem. In the beginning it was all good. It can still be good if only we try to outdo one another in loving. God loves us. Isn't this motive enough to love one another? And the sequence is still the same. God loves us first in every situation, all the time, and with relentless passion. God does not have to adjust. He is love.

---

1. Erich Fromm. *The Art of Loving* (New York: Bantam Books, 1970) 111.

Life begets life. Would it not be grand if love begot love in the same way? Then again, would not that automatic response water down love as a gift that is freely offered? This would keep us from being able to celebrate the most exhilarating and liberating experience of all, a free mutual love between God and ourselves. We can do it. We have been told how. "As the Father has loved me, so have I loved you," to which Jesus adds a little love note, "Abide in my love" (John 15:9). "I love you" may be the three most important words in our vocabulary, but they mean little until we include the more important word "as." We either love as Jesus does or we do not love at all.

Love always involves another. A lover can never be a spectator. That is why we are never mere objects of God's love or why in degraded love people can become just playthings. Where in the New Testament does Jesus treat people as just "out there"? It is absolutely impossible for God who loves himself not to be involved with himself and with us. In Erich Fromm's *The Art of Loving*, the word to be emphasized is art. Francis Henry Taylor, the museum curator, said, "The one quality denied a work of art throughout the ages is privacy. Unless participation is allowed the spectator, it becomes a hopeless riddle and ceases to be a work of art at all."[2]

Imagine if Jesus appeared on the earth merely as a spectator or a tourist, a sight-seer. How sterile any account of his life would be. It would be like showing slides of a vacation to someone already bored with life. Just by being born into this world, Jesus involved himself in our lives. He brought out the lovable in people. He even died that we might live. He practiced what Isaiah predicted, "What more was there to do for my vineyard, that I have not done in it?" (5:4)

Is there anything that Jesus fails to do for us? If we are hated, he teaches us how to handle it with humility. If we are bedridden with pain, he shows us how to take up our cross as he did his and follow him. If we are laden with sins, he embraces me and invites me to whisper them to him so that he can forgive them. Whatever we need to be healthier, happier, and holier, he stands ready to help. He does more. He comes after us as though afraid he might lose sight of us.

---

2. Sarel Eimerl. *World of Giotto* (New York: Time Inc. [Time-Life Library of Art], 1967) 8.

In the thirteenth century, for the first time in art history, the paintings of Giotto projected people, emotions, and themes so that they became shared experiences for viewers. By grouping people in the lower half of his paintings, the beholder could look at and into them at eye level, an involvement level, an engrossed level. The English art critic John Ruskin wrote that Giotto "painted what no man could look upon without being the better for it."[3] He did not paint the Madonna, St. Joseph, and Christ, but momma, papa, and the baby.[4] We should apply this insight the next time we look at a crucifix. We will surely be the better for the attempt. What an artist God is! He created us so that when two hearts are aglow with love for God and each other, there is an involvement level beyond which there is none more ecstatic.

No activity can begin with such high expectations and end with so much disaster as loving. As Christians we should not be pessimistic, but we hear and read of so much failure in loving: broken homes, shattered marriages, vows, oaths, promises solemnly made but not kept. This is most alarming, but it is not the full picture. All around us, with much less publicity, do we not see genuine sacrifice, people rising above themselves in support of one another, emptying themselves as they meet a neighbor's need to be loved? We do not have to look around us. How often do people try to love us as Jesus loves us. All around us are walking valentines. They attest to the joy of loving us as God so happily and unselfishly loves himself.

Love is the one thing no one can pilfer from us, like the joy Jesus said no man can take from us. Love is also the one thing we can constantly give and become the richer by giving. When we withhold love we rob ourselves. When we refuse to love or be loved, we invite misery and loneliness into our lives. The saddest commentary of all is that, but for an adjustment, it need not be. Unless we change, accommodate, turn it all around, we will never know that God loves himself because he loves us.

_____

3. *Ibid.* 183.
4. *Ibid.* 10.

5

Faith in God

One day, after listening in earnest to Jesus, the apostles begged him, "Increase our faith" (Luke 17:5). Somewhat mandatory in tone, the request was certainly reasonable and no doubt pleasing to the Lord. It even approached formal prayer. Supposedly, the apostles had witnessed and wanted the faith that Jesus placed in his Father. Jesus then instructed the apostles what genuine faith was all about.

St. Paul corrected the notion that faith is a magical muscle or an occult power that comes from the outside. "I can do all things in him who strengthens me" (Phil 4:13). Who more than Paul knew that faith did not exist in a vacuum. Faith is not out there. Faith is not something that we get as a gift. It is an "it" only when we talk about it in general. Faith is a way of living with God, and on earth it is life itself. Our whole person shares in God.

Many call Abraham our "father in faith." Faith is a form of life that one can transmit to those who come after, as did Abraham to the Jews. As a gift from God, faith has to do with the Spirit breathing this gift in us. It is a spiritual breath-giving. Having received this gift, we can be wholeheartedly alive. An increase in believing brings about a more intense living. All that we do is more spirited, alive, joyful, and pleasing to God. Faith is "in him who strengthens," in Jesus who came that we "may have life, and have it abundantly" (John 10:10). That life we can have now by believing in God.

Jesus never asks a complicated, mind-boggling question. Jesus is never nettled by a heckling response. He is angry at times, yes, but in his anger composed. "If we are faithless, he remains faithful — for he cannot deny himself" (2 Tim 2:13). Completely loyal and totally reliable is the faith of Jesus in us. "While I was with them . . . I have guarded them" (John 17:12).

Indispensable to courageous living is steadfast belief. If any one of us aspires to become great, that is, pleasing to God, it will only

25

happen if we live out our faith. Once St. Thomas had overcome his doubt about the risen Lord, he believed completely. "My Lord and my God!" (John 20:28).

God is not an easy companion to walk with, but, if we live with faith in him and let him lead, let him set the pace, what seems burdensome can become joyous. St. Francis of Assisi wrote: "When I was in sin, the sight of lepers nauseated me beyond measure; but then God himself led me into their company, and I had pity on them. When I had once become acquainted with them, what previously nauseated me became a source of spiritual and physical consolation for me."[1]

All truly holy men and women of God experience some bitterness, but they emerge from their trials and taste sweetness. They exemplify growth in faith. They too beg Jesus, "Increase our faith."

One reason why many fail to live up to faith is their lack of a strong understanding of it. Faith is a gift of the Holy Spirit, but this virtue is not something boxed and wrapped. If it were, faith could come and go without increasing or diminishing the joy and the courage of living. If a gift is not a gift until someone accepts it, then faith is not faith until someone lives it. Until that happens we have only academic chatter, theological speculation, so much catechetical mishandling of it. Until it is lived in us, until every word and trust is in God, there is no faith, no gift. Seeing may be believing but believing is living. When that believing is in God, then we are sharing to the full.

Jesus one day enlightened his apostles about faith, "If you had faith as a grain of mustard seed, you could say to this sycamine tree, 'Be rooted up, and be planted in the sea,' and it would obey you" (Luke 17:6). In Matthew's Gospel, instead of a tree, it is a mountain, an image even more emphatic. Jesus was telling the apostles that he would rather root up mountains than change his mind. That is the holding power of faith even though that faith be the size of the smallest perceptible object in Jesus' time, a mustard seed.

The condition of faith can never be duty alone. Jesus told his apostles:

---

1. *St. Francis of Assisi*, ed. Marion Habig (Chicago: Franciscan Herald Press, 1973) 67.

Will any one of you, who has a servant plowing or keeping sheep, say
to him when he has come in from the field, "Come at once and sit down
at table"? Will he not rather say to him, "Prepare supper for me, and
gird yourself and serve me, till I eat and drink; and afterward you shall
eat and drink"? Does he thank the servant because he did what was
commanded? So you also, when you do all that is commanded you,
say, "We are unworthy servants; we have only done what was our
duty" (Luke 17:7-10).

The Pharisees demonstrated beyond any doubt their faithfulness to
rules and regulations. They became immovable mountains. How difficult it is to put faith in such people.

"Hence I remind you to rekindle the gift of God that is within
you through the laying on of my hands" (2 Tim 1:6). St. Paul is refer-
ring to the receiving of the Holy Spirit and his gifts. Unless there is a
spark, and in this instance the Holy Spirit, there is no way to stir
anything into a flame. Nothing will be enkindled without his love.
However, our action is needed to fan that spark into a glowing faith.
Without our response that spark will become a dying ember. The
Holy Spirit never imposes himself. God does not apply force. He
waits for faith in him.

A decline of faith in personal immortality has probably been the
most important political fact of the last one hundred years. We are in
the middle of a faith crisis in which Satan has had more than a walk-
on part. He would have us see sin as limited to vice, to conduct, to
morality. Subtly he eases God from center stage. No longer is it a
failure to fully trust in a personal God. No longer is faith in God but
a safety-precaution decision about him. What an adjustment this
calls for!

It was the faith of the poor, the "little ones," which occasioned
in the gospels the first glad news of Jesus' resurrection. Mary anticipated this in her *Magnificat*. She herself was the smallest of the "little
ones" who place themselves at the disposition of God. Another poor
one, the Little Flower of Jesus, Thérèse, at age twenty-three said
joyfully on her deathbed, "I love everything God in his goodness
sends me."[2] It took a lot of faith to say this. Especially when dying
was part of everything. On another occasion Thérèse exclaimed, "All

---

2. Thomas Taylor. *St. Thérèse of Lisieux* (New York: P. J. Kenedy & Sons, 1926) 233.

the way to heaven is heaven." Only those who walk that way with faith in God have this experience. What a loyal daughter of Abraham! Her faith gave her the right to call him "father."

What is our kinship to Abraham? A hearsay acquaintance? A distant relative? Must we admit, "Abraham who?" We might take our cue from the apostles and request as they did, "Lord, we too! Increase our faith." Then we should add, "Give us the courage to believe in God so that we too can claim Abraham as 'our father in faith.'" All it takes is the accommodating prayer of petition. Pray it from the heart and believe. Childlike trust in God means we are his children. It also means that "Whatever is born of God overcomes the world; and this is the victory that overcomes the world, our faith" (1 John 5:4).

6

Faith in God Means Faith in People

Abraham Lincoln's memorable speech at Gettysburg is part of the nation's heritage. Practically every elementary student memorizes all or part of it. The address was so short that the official photographer had no time to adjust his camera for a picture. Preceding the President was Edward Everett, former president of Harvard, secretary of state, senator, and a prestigious orator. After people realized how great Lincoln's words were, Everett wrote: "I should be glad if I could flatter myself that I came as near the central idea of the occasion in two hours as you did in two minutes."[1] Lincoln's "that government of the people, by the people, and for the people, shall not perish from the earth" summarized that central idea.

It should not take two hours, or even two minutes, to arrive at the central idea of our God-created existence, the worship of God and the love of neighbor. If people want to be dedicated, consecrated and hallowed, there must be faith in all peoples. Without it every government will eventually perish, regardless of how much it is "of and by the people."

To add or to detract from this faith in people is not above our power and will. Faith in people is of the substance of Jesus' mission on earth. Patterned after his faith in us, our mission is the unfinished work which he advanced by dying for us. St. Paul made this cause the central work of his mission to the Gentiles. "So if there is any encouragement in Christ, any incentive of love, any participation in the Spirit, any affection and sympathy, complete my joy of being of the same mind, having the same love, being in full accord and of one mind" (Phil 2:1-2).

---

1. Svend Petersen, *The Gettysburg Addresses: The Story of Two Orations* (New York: Frederick Ungar Publishing Co., 1963) 165.

Let us evaluate that attitude, not with a lot of propositions but in the real person of the wealthy tax collector Zacchaeus. One day Jesus passed through Jericho, which was Zacchaeus' home town, en route to Jerusalem. Despised, distrusted, shunned by his neighbors, Zacchaeus hears that Jesus is approaching. Short of stature, he scampers up a sycamore tree to better see Jesus. Perched at that vantage point, little does he suspect that the route Jesus is taking will be right through his heart. Before the sun sets he will publicly confess his faults, promise to make good, and even break bread with Jesus.

Zacchaeus was alone in that tree. No photographer was there to take this unusual picture, but sooner than it takes to adjust any camera Jesus said, "Zacchaeus, make haste and come down; for I must stay at your house today" (Luke 19:5). Zacchaeus then bounded out of the tree. He who had run ahead of the crowd was now hurrying toward Jesus. Even more, he was leading Jesus into his home. Oh, there were murmurings and rumblings from the crowd, but all Zacchaeus heard was, "Zacchaeus, come down." It mattered only that he had regained self-respect. This was central to the reality.

To lose or lessen our faith in people is to slacken our trust in God. God and people are of the same person-package — emphatically so from the day Mary gave birth to her son Jesus Christ, the Son of God. It does matter that Zacchaeus had faith in Jesus, and it is critically important that Jesus had confidence in Zacchaeus.

Is there more violence today or are we more aware of it? Have the media, with their instantaneous coverage of crime, given rise to a wholesale cynicism of the human family? Is the boom in the burglar alarm trade also alerting us to a serious people problem? I believe so. Trustworthiness itself is on trial. Now, as never before, we are compelled to answer the question: What is there about people that places a demand on our faith? And here is the answer.

We all need that support, *batah* in Hebrew. We all need a haven or *hasah* where we can take refuge. These common needs forbid converting faith into a kind of speculation. Even if people should betray *batah* and mock *hasah*, we all have support from Jesus. "As thou didst send me into the world, so I have sent them into the world. And for their sake I consecrate myself, that they also may be consecrated in truth" (John 17:18-19). Today Jesus is consecrating the faithful in truth. Today around the world countless thousands are committing themselves to the Father through him in the Lord's Prayer. Someone will always hear, "Come down; for I must stay at your house today." And that person will respond with faith.

We either risk faith in others or continue our on-going education in sour cynicism. Derived from *kyonikos* in Greek, "cynic" means doglike. It refers to a little dog who snips and snaps regardless of how genuine and gentle the greeting. A cynic bares his or her teeth in disgust when the same teeth could flash a smile. It is no picnic to be a cynic. It takes practice to act and react with sarcasm, to use criticism like a cutlass. At home only with darkened clouds that have no silver linings, the cynic prefers a life that is gloomed over and doomed out.

A Japanese proverb teaches that the threshold is the highest mountain in the world. If so, the highest threshold must be that experience whereby we cross over into concern for each other. It takes a heap of faith to leap that threshold. The parable of the Good Samaritan reminds us that we do not structure our own thresholds. The very next person we meet is that threshold. We do not decide who he or she will be. Whoever they are, they are Christ. What a blanket adjustment this entails! What an open-ended accommodation! Jesus did not decide to love us. We are his decision. We are his love. He is, as only he can be, love. Love is central to everything good. His threshold is ours.

Keep faith in God and people, and it will keep you. Once we lose it, we lose everything. We stifle life itself. Then love becomes hate, life becomes death, friends are enemies, God is gone. Robert Browning said it well in "A Death in the Desert":

> This is death and the sole death
>   When a man's loss
> Comes to him from his gain;
>   From knowledge ignorance,
> And lack of love
>   From love made manifest.[2]

---

2. Robert Browning. *The Poetic and Dramatic Works of Robert Browning*, vol. 4 (New York: H. Houghton and Co., 1887) 26.

Ironically, those who killed Jesus, who is life, were in search of a better life. But his faith in us would not die nor would it end with his death. Having risen and crossed the threshold of his tomb, he now stands at our threshold and knocks. He will enter only upon invitation. Only if we let him share our life will we be ready to risk our trust in others.

7

The Honest Question

There is just one way to do business with God: the honest way. To be dishonest with God, who can neither deceive nor be deceived, is to cheat oneself. Dishonesty guarantees the truth that a liar knows he is telling a lie. The teller lives the lie, which is rather suicidal behavior.

It was on a day of deception that the Sadducees, who were aristocratic clerics, deceitfully questioned Jesus. The question concerned resurrection from the dead, which they considered an outlandish teaching. They hoped to trap Jesus:

> "Teacher, Moses wrote for us that if a man's brother dies, having a wife but no children, the man must take the wife and raise up children for his brother. Now there were seven brothers; the first took a wife, and died without children; and the second and the third took her, and likewise all seven left no children and died. Afterward the woman also died. In the resurrection, therefore, whose wife will the woman be? For the seven had her as a wife." (Luke 20:27-33).

Theirs was a dishonest, self-serving question asked with no intention of expecting an answer. They simply wanted to push a pernicious point, to nettle Jesus. They were downright deceivers because they themselves did not believe in the resurrection from the dead. The Sadducees did not ask the honest question because their attitudes were fixed, their minds closed, their intentions encased. Jesus knew they were experimenting with him, using him, exploiting him. This is the way the self-righteous act.

Many are the mysteries of life, but faith is broader and deeper then knowledge. Indeed, faith is a form of superior knowledge. What if we all had perfect knowledge on earth and could make the lie impossible? What next? Like Alexander the Great, who supposedly grieved because he had no more territory to conquer, we too would become disgusted grist ready for the boredom mill. The very risk at honesty makes for a venturesome life and our faith a real adventure. The Sadducees failed to ask the question in good faith. They could not ask it in truth. Their question was deceptive and boring.

To get engrossed in a thrilling novel and then in the middle of it have someone blurt out the surprise ending is disappointing. To watch a movie with a companion who insists on babbling a commentary is irksome. Well, God does nothing of this sort. He is full of surprises, some of which he will not reveal until the end of our life.

We believe there is a surprise ending to our life's story just as there was surprise at the beginning of our Christian experience. God sent his Son not just to spring a surprise but that we may live life to the full and prepare for the surprise ending. Nowhere in the Gospels do we read of Jesus spoiling the plot. He did not spoil it for Martha and Mary when their brother died. Just for waiting, Martha and Mary tasted the best of honesty and truth at the last. Jesus did not spoil it for the apostles. Patiently honest with them, he let them linger in fear and wallow in doubt so that when he rose from the tomb their surprise was beyond describing.

There was no surprise for the dogged Sadducees in the answer Jesus gave to their dishonest question. In gentlemanly fashion, Jesus reminded them how ignorant they were of Scripture. He gave them time to ponder, then replied, "Now he is not God of the dead, but of the living" (Luke 20:38). This statement is loaded with answers, provided we ask honest questions, such as "What does God mean to me in this world?" or "What kind of a surprise awaits me in heaven?"

While the Sadducees were dishonest enough to deceive Jesus, we have to be honest enough to admit that he is the Truth. Otherwise our condition is worse than theirs. Our problem is not theirs, life after death, but a truthful living before dying. The honest question really is: Do we make an earnest attempt to search for the truth as God has revealed it and his Church has handed on to us? More honestly, do we even suspect that the truth, in answer to our most demanding questions, is harvest-ready in the Bible? Prayer? Sacraments? In the silence of a room, the quiet of a chapel, in a peaceful countryside? Are our minds and hearts open to the truth in whatever form it comes, however painful? Are they open for business, our Father's business? If so, to what extent do we honestly go about it?

We all know it is sometimes more difficult to ask the honest question sincerely than it is to give the answer truthfully.

Truth, as Aristotle taught it, is the conformity of our minds with the real world as it presents itself to us. The Semites of the Old Testament regarded truth as a religious experience. It was either a lived fidelity to the covenant God made with his people or later, with the appearance of Jesus, a shared discipleship with him. Jesus always asks honest questions, some quite painful, so that we might enjoy truthful living. He always involves himself in the answer as the one person capable of making life a happy religious experience.

For St. John the Apostle, salvation is never a matter of human activity that follows upon divine inspiration. This for him is not the meaning of faith or truth. Rather, truth is the acceptance of God's love which continues to accomplish its surprise in those who believe. We do not arrive at truth as we arrive at grandma's house. We accept it, embrace it, live it, love it, enjoy it. Truth is not an "it" but a "him." Truth is very personal. Otherwise we could never grow in truth. Honesty then is not assent to truth as a matter of policy. It is an obedient surrender to Jesus who as Truth becomes our way of life. Without this honesty there is no discipleship. There are no happy surprises. There is only toying with the truth as the Sadducees did.

Honesty is more than the perfectly balanced arms of a measuring scale. Honesty is nothing less than, and above all, Jesus Christ. "I am the way" . . . (John 14:6), Jesus told us. Honesty is Jesus with arms stretched on the cross to shape us to the truth. He died that we might experience his love and know him as the truth that makes us free. Truth does not take away physical pain but it does liberate. Jesus does not offer us the pain of his cross but the love that led him there. He is always honest enough to tell us that there will always be pain, distress, and suffering. He is truthful enough to add that a great surprise awaits those who live by his truth. The heroic dissidents in Russia today would rather die than forsake the truth. They should move us to appreciate the truth we take so much as a matter of policy.

Finally, here is a reminder about the personality of the lie. Just as we can grow in the truth, so can we stunt ourselves if we live by the lie. One day, in the Temple area where he was accustomed to teach, Jesus rebuked the crowd that was conniving to kill him because his message found no hearing among them. Fearlessly he chastised them: "You are of your father the devil, and your will is to do your father's desires. . . . When he lies, he speaks according to his own nature . . . . But because I tell the truth, you do not believe me" (John 8:44-45). What followed was one of the most honest questions ever asked, "Which of you convicts me of sin?" (8:46) Jesus confronted Satan himself. Just as Jesus did not sell out the truth when the devil tempted him in the desert, here he refused him any accommodation whatsoever. Truth never compromises.

Our world is not the "plenitude of evil" as the Gnostics would have it. Evil tendencies, yes. Mendacious-mindedness, sure. Deviousness, no doubt. To offset these sins is precisely why Jesus came to live among us. He came to expose Satan as the "father of lies," as one who prefers the lie to the truth, darkness to the light. No child is ever begotten of Satan, but not a few of us are in need of rescue from him. We need to be set free. We need to know Jesus as the Truth. We need to know that honesty is not a policy but a person. The sooner we adjust to the person who is Jesus Christ, by sharing the truth, dealing honestly with all of life's activity, the sooner will we enjoy God's gift of freedom.

8

Me, a Prophet?

God calls us to handle many chores. He doesn't use institutions, organizations, parliaments, senate chambers. He uses individuals. God is always personal. He phrases his mission simply in the words, "I am sending you." Our temperaments, dispositions, personalities don't really count. God chooses us just as we are, wherever we are. In the Old Testament, missioners of God were the prophets. In the New, we are the missioners.

In the biblical sense a prophet does not decipher the future or dig out truths the past tries to hide. Such things are only signs that put God's stamp on his mission. The prophet has nothing to do with spectaculars. His uniqueness comes not from himself but from God's having chosen him. He is not the mission but the missioner. He is not just a storyteller who talks about God. He is an unsettling, disturbing person who speaks for him.

As one whom God inspired, the prophet gave substance to the Bible. What he said mattered. Even more, it mattered who he was. He was a voice that firmed up a faltering faith. Rarely sentimental, the tone of his message was frequently childlike and caressing. Often he brought courage and consolation to the wounded. Just as often, he was a scourge to the oppressive. He forbade his audience to be indifferent to his urgings. He never let his listeners forget. Remembering, more than recognizing, was at the core of his mission. Since the mission was God's but the temperament his, he repeatedly shrank before the towering task God called him to—personally. Hesitant in response, the prophet overcame fright with a resolute No! to popular opinion and an exclamatory Yes! to his unpredictable God.

On the sultry day that Jesus talked to the Samaritan woman at the well in Shechem and exposed her crazy-quilted past, she calmly replied, "Sir, I perceive that you are a prophet" (John 4:19). To her he was not yet the Messiah, as she would confess him to be before the sun had set. But he was no longer a passing Jew, a stranger, or ordinary traveler. He was a prophet! Her contact with the history of the Jews must have introduced her to the prophets. And now a prophet sat beside her at the edge of the well and at the fringe of her heart. "I perceive that you are a prophet." One can sense the inflection, a subtle insistence that he say more. She was beginning to trust the purpose of every genuine prophet. "Think not that I have come to abolish the law and the prophets; I have come not to abolish them but to fulfill them" (Matt 5:17). He is the Father's Word, eternal Truth. For him to be is to speak. He is news, the Good News, the Best News. Whenever he speaks, it is to our deepest needs. Whenever we listen, it should be in the same way as prophets listened to God.

The prophet Jeremiah rebuked his contemporaries because "Their ears are closed . . . behold the word of the Lord is to them an object of scorn" (6:10). John reminds us that if the word of God is to become glad tidings, there is one condition mankind has to meet: "He who is of God hears the words of God . . ." (8:47). Every word. Not just the self-interesting word. Every word.

The word of God has a personality. As God created the birds to fly and man to think and love, so God's word exists to communicate himself. Unless there is a speaking—and a listening—there is no exchange. Never did the word of God come into his own more than when he spoke to Mary, the Virgin Mother of Jesus. Her Son beatified her on earth for listening to that word, "Blessed rather are those who hear the word of God and keep it" (Luke 11:28). Little wonder she later came into the honor that was her due as the queen of prophets. As Moses heard God on Sinai, Mary absorbed him in her attentive heart. She was the daughter of Israel who listened. Mary was quiet by disposition, as though any speaking might interrupt the listening. There was only so much time to listen—but all eternity to sing her magnificent love.

Me, a prophet? I wouldn't dare, any more than the woman of Shechem ever dreamt she would be sitting within a shadow's length of the prophet. God called the prophets in the Old Testament to remind their listeners of his covenant, and theirs, while preparing them for the coming of the Messiah. Who speaks for God now that he is with us? God's method is still people. There had better be some prayerful listening lest we become deaf and dumb prophets, living contradictions of our calling. Jesus once replied to the Pharisee who asked him to rebuke his disciples, "I tell you, if these were silent, the very stones would cry out" (Luke 19:40).

What is there about our times that places a demand on more prophets who willingly and courageously speak for God? Man's unsatisfied search for ultimate meaning is the pathology of our age. It is something each of us must find. Helping us are those who find meaning in their lives, live up to it, and verbalize it to others. This is adjustment at its charitable best. This could very well be the love whereby one lays down his life for a friend. This, too, is a mission no less imperative than that of the great prophets, including the last and greatest — John the Baptist.

One of the deeper forms of prophecy is the voice of our conscience. In listening to it, we fulfill the genuine condition for conversion. For that to happen we must enter into the cave of the heart, where we gradually acknowledge our real worth. There silence shouts. There we begin to see the hidden self in what Gregory of Nyssa called the "luminous darkness." In the dungeon darkness we hear as never before. We learn to speak to and listen to God before speaking for him as his prophet.

Just as we live the deepest moments of love in silent communication, so too the modern prophet can broadcast his message nonverbally. Speaking is but one manner of communicating. The Word was made flesh before he spoke. If the ancient prophets called for conversion by challenging the people to remember the glorious events in which God came to their aid, then ours is the mission to remind one another that God became man and is still with us as our Savior. This mission is the call of every modern prophet.

The best influence comes by good example. What we say must be backed by what we are. In a word-weary world it is possible that we may have evangelized God's influence out of existence. Too much speaking can be canceled out by too little listening. The overkill of words can render even God anonymous.

Athletes use the term "body English" to define certain twists and movements, such as the swish of the baseball bat, a backhand tennis return, or the liquid-smooth swing of a tee shot. Then why not "soul" English? Or personal-influence English? The way we share, the manner of prayer, the kind of love. Real influence lacks control. We do not manipulate it. To be *holy* means to *be* holy. We must be ourselves after letting God make us what we are. One cannot exact more than this from any modern prophet. Jesus said, "He who abides in me, and I in him, he it is that bears much fruit" (John 15:5). Then the person is the pronouncement and proclamation. Then the word of God is active and alive. The mission of the prophet becomes unquestionably clear. That mission then becomes nothing less than to be Christ for others. But hold it! Lest we become too cozy about it all, listen to the reminder of all genuine prophets: It takes more courage, generosity, and sacrifice to be the message than it ever does to speak it.

The true prophet concedes all control to God and his grace. But this is not mere passivism. The loudest of actions must be a listening with the heart to the inspiring word of God. St. Paul ranked prophecy above the gift of tongues (1 Cor 14:1). "Think before you speak."

Me, a prophet? If some say "why?" we must say "why not?" Whether in words or works, we all tell each other something. The world is alive with inter-communication. What is it we are attempting to say? To whom are we listening? If that whom is Jesus, then the world will take on a more serene look.

9

We Are a Priestly People

A few years ago, after an operation, I lay in the recovery room awaiting return to consciousness. As I emerged from the anesthesia, I heard a faint voice, presumably that of a nurse, say, "This one is a priest."

What does the term "priest" signify? In the Old Testament times, the different tribes had their own priests. Temples did not stand, priests as specially chosen with any formality or amidst ceremony did not exist. Altars and sacrifices, of course, did abound. With Moses, God chose the tribe of Levi and set it apart for worship duties. The meaning of the priesthood deepened. Eventually kings became patrons of the priesthood and Jerusalem the center of worship. Gradually the priesthood assumed respected authority, became a guide to the nation, and took on the form of an office with a presiding high priest, as is mentioned in the New Testament during the trial of Jesus.

Levites presented to God the offerings of his people. In turn these priests relayed to God's people his blessings. They also guarded the Ark, shepherded his flock, presided during great feasts, relived the great memories such as the Exodus experience, and became scholars of the Torah, the Law. But the one dominating purpose for which God summoned this tribe was to offer sacrifice for all people.

In the New Testament times, each of us shares in the priesthood of Jesus Christ, who is both God and man, both priest and sacrifice. At his invitation, by reason of his call, we share this sacred duty with him. We too are chosen for all people. We are priests. We are set apart. We are holy priests.

Up to now it all reads so positive. However, even though the tradition of the priesthood in the time of Moses was kept alive, priests do profane the liturgy, succumb to pagan influence, buck the prophets, exploit the Torah, and pursue selfish interests. They compromise hard-nosed zeal and saintly ambition. In reaction prophets excoriate them as do other priests. All this instructs us that the priesthood does not guarantee immunity from the frailties of human nature. In fact, the more priestly the person, the more fragile the calling, the more vulnerable the priestly life. And yet the wisdom of it all. God calls us to the priesthood not because of our strengths but because of our weaknesses. Our greatest strength is to confide in him our weaknesses while trusting in his strength.

To share in the priesthood of Jesus to the full, now offering him in sacrifice, now become one with him in the offering, now for the glory of God, now for all the people, what a joyful experience! Even the pain felt, the patience expended, the pressures incurred are part of that joy — they too are sacrifice. All of it is positive, perhaps one of the most positive efforts we can make in this world.

As Jesus goes about his Father's business, he never claims for himself the title of priest. The Father does not send him to give him honors but to be the priest, be the sacrifice. As God and man he is the perfect priest who offers the perfect gift to his Father. As God became man he makes it possible for us to share in his priesthood.

St. Paul's Letter to the Hebrews is the first Christian sermon on record. Written to rouse and tighten a slackening faith in God, it profiles the priesthood of Jesus Christ. It contains beautiful sentiments concerning the priesthood. "Jesus Christ is the same yesterday and today and for ever" (13:8). The "and" embraces all time while holding on to the eternal. It affirms Jesus' priesthood and ours in a concelebrated ritual of life on earth while we await with expectant hope the unimaginable celebration in heaven.

"This one is a priest." The nurse may have said it as a passing remark or simply because the medical chart listed me so. Not so these words, "You are a priest for ever . . ." (Ps 110:4). Ours is a priestly life. We are the sacrifice. We are Jesus Christ in this world. We are the celebrants of the Eucharist. We are the living Scripture. We are the living reminders of the Exodus experience, not just an instant replay of it.

There is no irresponsibility so damaging as the failure to answer the call of God to the priesthood, unless it be the failure to listen to the call itself. Just for there being one less priest, how much good never will be done? Certainly it takes courage. Of course it can happen only with faith. As always the initiative is God's. None of us can plead ignorance as did Isaac when he asked his father, "Where is the lamb for a burnt offering?" All of us can give Abraham's answer: "God will provide himself the lamb for a burnt offering, my son" (Gen 22:7-8).

Many things that we do by ourselves make us happy—hobbies, studies, games, prayers. However, some of our happiest experiences also come by invitation: a teacher expects an answer to a very difficult question and we have it; a vagrant mumbles a sincere plea for food and we share ours; a youngster afraid to ask needs attention and we give it. Should not then the happiest of all experiences be that in which God invites us to a special mission, calls us to his priesthood, and we accept it? If the call is a once-and-for-all call to the priesthood, then the answer should be the same. Just as we grow in the love of God, so should we grow in the priesthood. It is a great honor because we are honored by God. We are his choice.

We all like to be singled out in any commendable situation. Unless pride or lack of interest dominate the heart, we respond with humility. If only that humility which was with us in the beginning would persist throughout our lives as priests, we would be the living sacrifices and have pleasing substance to offer to God for his people. We would then happily share the priesthood of Jesus Christ as he so desires to enjoy ours.

Unless we are familiar with the names in the genealogy of St. Matthew, we just might not realize that four names are those of women: Tamar, Rahab, Bathsheba, and Ruth. Each was instrumental in revealing God's mind on earth. God calls us not because of our strength but because of our weaknesses. Inspired by these valiant women, let us become worthy instruments of God. Admitting shortcomings is one thing; doing something about them is another. Where there are lapses, let there be remorse and rededication. Where the people have been let down, let there be renewed ambition. Where prayer has been reluctant and empty of faith, let there be words and songs of proclamation.

We are priests. If God called us, he will sustain us. He knows what he is doing. We are certain that he has called us. "For God is not so unjust as to overlook your work and the love which you showed for his sake in serving the saints . . ." (Heb 6:10). In asking for his continued blessing, do not ever forget that by being good priests we *are* that blessing—forever!

10

The Call to Conversion

Only to the extent that we understand religious conversion do we enjoy a happy and wholesome life. There can be no shallow adjustment here since there is no conversion worthwhile unless it is a turning of the heart. Not easy. When it is a turning of the heart, conversion is a spiritual rebirth, regeneration, and rehabilitation. Conversion is a resurrection term. When we convert we reckon our lives not by days and years but by a series of ceaseless, happy returns to God.

Whenever God calls, even though the call be indirect, it is always a call to himself. The response in faith is one of conversion, whether it is, as for all of us, from sin; or, as for one of us, Mary, toward God. It makes no difference whether we define conversion as a changing of a route, a fixing of the heart, or the seeking of God, the meaning is the same, a facing up to God in full surrender while fencing out pride.

In the Old Testament judges administered justice severely. Sinners broke the bond of union and communion with God. The expected penalty was death. They gave up any hope of redemption. The guilty could hand themselves over to divine chastisement and beg for pardon. In this world they had no one who could justify or exonerate them.

After his serious sin, David handed himself over to God, turned to him with this confession, "Lo, I have sinned, and I have done wickedly; but these sheep, what have they done? Let thy hand, I pray thee, be against me and against my father's house" (2 Sam 24:17). We fail to appreciate the severe penalty due sin, as David did, unless we understand the depth and breadth of the separation caused by a denial of God. Centuries of narrow Christian attitude have belittled the enormity of even a single sin.

Old Testament theology defined sin as "missing the mark," as when a hasty traveler loses his way. Other meanings included "overstepping"and "rebelling." As originally used, the Latin *peccatum*, or the English *peccadillo* did not mean anything immoral. More correctly it was a word which translated the phrase, "What a pity!" Not until late Judaism did the notion of sin become legalistic in meaning. How repeatedly Jesus attacked this meaning of sin. As early as the prophet Amos, sin was never understood solely as a violation of a law. Its face value was a fired-up, hard-hearted rebellion against God's will. Any conversion entailed grief over sins committed, repentance of them, and a raw-boned satisfaction for them. The return to God was not a cozy, conditioned response, but a sincere contriteness of heart that broke up the very core of a bad deed or habit.

Conversion and covenant are related words. Only in the light of God's covenant with Moses and with his people can we evaluate sin as "missing the mark" and conversion as a most happy return to God. On Mount Sinai God did not initiate any bilateral contract with us. His is a pact of loyalty and love, not of justice as we commonly know contracts to be. God's love is forever merciful and forgiving. Whatever our response, or the lack of it, God is always love. Who would ever dream of such an accommodation? This is further evidence why God's way is not our way.

To rebel against such a covenant is an ingratitude which obviously more than oversteps the delicate bounds of etiquette. It is the clay yelling at the potter, "I have no need of you"; the creature smirking at the Creator, "Who asked you?"; Peter denying Jesus with defiance and with shoulders squared, "I do not know the man" (Matt 26:74). In return for love there is hate, for mercy pride, for the shared joy the sickening feeling that saps the souls of those who never understand God's overture of love on Sinai, let alone Jesus' love on Calvary. Little wonder the last words of Jesus rebound off the surface of stony hearts, "Father, forgive them; for they know not what they do" (Luke 23:34). Penance and repentance are all but impossible when anyone refuses to acknowledge the one to whom he must turn or the sins from which he must convert.

Sin has built-in judgment. Sin carries its own consequences. It is not the residual by-product of some ill-conceived and ill-willed deed. Sin is not the absence of good. This would make it comfortable to live with. For the Semite sin was a positive reality which continued to exist and remain until the sinner admitted it, confessed it, and accepted God's mercy for it. In the book of Numbers, sin and its effects are so paralleled as to appear synonymous. "But if you will not do so, behold, you have sinned against the Lord; and be sure your sin will find you out" (32:23).

Because sin is positive we can reasonably understand why an entire community suffers for the guilt of a few or even one. The broken family, the aborted marriage, the boy and girl who split from their parents, the friend who becomes an enemy are some examples of the permanence of sin. This means communal conversion is here to stay, and communal penance will remain as long as anyone sins. Here is the reason why the penitential prayer of the compassionate prophet Jeremiah is as urgent today as it was centuries ago: "Correct me, O Lord, but in just measure; not in thy anger, lest thou bring me to nothing" (10:24).

The sin of apostasy unmasks some terrible insights. Such a sin does not disturb the indifferent consciences of so many who make faith the equivalent of opinion or theoretical judgment. The apostate with full deliberation decisively cuts himself off from the only source and substance of happiness, God. When the author of the Letter to the Hebrews insisted that it was practically impossible to convert those who turned away from God, after having once tasted and enjoyed his gifts, he anticipated what every good spiritual director knows from experience. An apostate does more than change his mind or divert his interest. He twists his entire life around 180 degrees. It is much more than an about-face. It is the heart beating to another drum. It is telling God, "For me you exist no more!" That is why anything less than loving God with the whole heart is already off the mark, missing the mark, laying the bedrock of another route.

Sin is broader than an immoral act, more than just a misdeed. Sin denies a personal God, offends all people, divides the sinner against himself. Nowhere does the Bible record sin as a form of fatalism. What some would suggest as fate is sin running its charted purpose. Only the free and contrite response to the grace of conversion can alter that trend.

There is perhaps no psalm more appropriate to guilt or that more fittingly supplies the sentiment for a contrite heart than David's prayer of repentance, the *Miserere*. When David pleaded, "Wash me thoroughly from my iniquity" (Ps 51:2), he literally meant "tread it out of me." In the Orient some people still wash clothes by flinging them against a rock in a shallow stream, stomping on them to make them clean. David was not using delicate language when he begged God to literally stomp his sins away and then create a new and clean heart for him.

In the middle of the *Miserere*, David also calls upon God to renew within him an upright spirit. This is really an earnest appeal for absolution. For the Israelite, the heart was more than a metaphor for deep-seated emotions. The Semite always thought about or said things in his heart rather than in his mind. David meant, in truth, create me anew; grant me another beginning, a fresh start. He was asking for something more resolute than the fickle change of mind that is often partner to a poor preparation for reconciliation or the timid promise which is forgotten soon after the words of absolution have faded away. If serious sin is radical, that is, committed whole-heartedly, sincere conversion must be just as intense. The God whom the sinner offends is the same God who desires that the sinner return. Without God there is no sinning. Only with God can there be a returning. So accommodating is God's mercy that for the sinner he has but one preoccupation, sharing that mercy.

The call to conversion was the most imperative of all calls in the mission of the last of the great prophets, John the Baptist. Of him Luke wrote, "And he will turn many of the sons of Israel to the Lord their God . . ." (Luke 1:16). In one nutshell sentence John translated his mission of mercy, "Repent, for the kingdom of heaven is at hand" (Matt 3:2). Absolution is available from Jesus. The forgiveness of Jesus is more than reprieve. When Jesus pardons he creates new hearts, turns us around, sets our sights on him so that we may never again want to miss the mark.

The call to conversion by Jesus was as unflagging as that of John. "I have not come to call the righteous, but sinners to repentance" (Luke 5:32). The flow of his mercy is always, "Come," "Follow me," "Learn of me." He stands at the door of our hearts to make all the forgive-and-forget accommodations. He patiently awaits our adjustment. With no allusions to penitential liturgies, with distrust in showy and theatrical signs, Jesus made it simple and human. The liturgies and the signs would come later. It boils down to a question which defines his mercy, a question he asked of two blind men near Jericho, "What do you want me to do for you?" (Matt 20:32). In restoring their sight there were no words, just the touch of his hand. That hand is still poised waiting to touch the other blind, the sinners. It takes a lot of heart for Jesus to continue to ask the same question. It also takes a lot of heart to answer it. When we do answer we say, "I too will return to my Father."

11

The Living Word of God

The phrase "word of God" is obviously a metaphor for us who believe in God and in the Word become flesh. The spoken word, as we hear it, we also attribute to Jesus Christ because he took upon himself our human nature. However, in the Old Testament, especially in the prophetic books, we read over and over again about the word of God, God speaking to Abraham, Moses, Samuel, and others. In its broadest sense the word of God means that God communicates with us just as prayer means that we communicate with God. Whether in the form of a vision, dream, inspiration, or as with Moses, face to face, we call all these the word of God.

What makes the word of God everlasting truth and joy is that practically every page and every word of Scripture communicates meaning and purpose to people of every geography and generation. However, this does not excuse us from studying the Semitic language and culture in which both Testaments first took root so that we may better understand and appreciate what God is saying to us.

God does not talk with people, and certainly Jesus never did merely to enlarge an inquisitive mind, broaden a vision, or deepen a curiosity. God never speaks to a person just to give some facts. When God speaks he reveals himself. If there were no revelation of God, we would have to insist, "Speak that we may know you." Since God does reveal himself through his word, his word is power, mercy, love, light, and truth. God's word is order within a formless wasteland. It is light that penetrates the dark, love that overcomes hatred, and truth that makes us free. God is the message, and the message is always about him.

God's word is communication, as men speak it, hear it, accept it, reject it, argue over it, speculate upon it, or take it to heart. The problem with us is not the way God speaks but what he says. We can even congratulate him for being consistent and logical. Just for having minds we can recognize this. As to what he says, we can accept God's word or refuse it. If he says, as he did say, "This is my Son, my Chosen; listen to him" (Luke 9:35), this is a pivotal word of God. Our hearts can listen to Jesus or turn him off because it is a matter of the heart and not the mind. If we are alive to the word of God and love what he says, even if the saying be harsh, then we will agree with the words of Jesus, "Man shall not live by bread alone, but by every word that proceeds from the mouth of God" (Matt 4:4). On these words hangs the tale of history.

By word of mouth we can communicate with one another without violating each other's freedom. Regardless of what we say or how we say it, we are free to turn a deaf ear. The same applies to God's word. It works in us only when we let it, when we listen to it. When we do, then hearing God becomes a form of prayer or even a song as it was for Moses, "Give ear, O heavens, and I will speak; and let the earth hear the words of my mouth. May my teaching drop as the rain, my speech distil as the dew . . ." (Deut 32:1-2). When Mary said, "Let it be to me according to your word" (Luke 1:38), she gave God the freedom to choose his words and herself as his mother. When the gentlemanly centurion confessed, "Lord, I am not worthy to have you come under my roof; but only say the word, and my servant will be healed" (Matt 8:8), he was telling Jesus that he was placing all his trust in his word. And when John with his mystical bent wrote, "And the Word became flesh and dwelt among us, full of grace and truth; we have beheld . . ." (1:14), he was saying that the Word, Jesus, is still alive. Our Lord is still communicating, God is still speaking.

Faith in God implies keeping our word; hope in him relying on his promised word; love for him taking his words and his Word, Jesus, and keeping them in our hearts. However, right from the beginning words were misused. The serpent tempted Adam and Eve with words, and both succumbed to their luring charm. They in turn took their cue from the serpent and used words to deceive, to lie, to evade, to accuse. How easy it is to take words and with them fake, perjure, offer false testimony. Again, we can take words and hammer them into pointed spears and wound others by cursing, scandalizing, alienating them. When the other is God himself or Jesus the Word, words uttered against them in pride or anger are blasphemy. St. Paul was keenly aware of the ways that we can prostitute words when he admitted, "For Christ did not send me to baptize but to preach the gospel, and not with eloquent wisdom, lest the cross of Christ be emptied of its power" (1 Cor 1:17). He was so terribly aware that in misappropriating the word of God he might himself become a castaway.

God's word is healing, but that word can be dividing. The very word "Jesus" divides the world into believers and unbelievers. God's word is solution as well as absolution. Indiscriminately available to all of us, it is never whispered to a favored few. God may be mysterious, but he is never secretive. The same word that is law is also love, harsh sounding to the moneychangers in the Temple, sweet sounding to those who listened with their hearts on the Mount of Beatitudes. God's word produces what it proclaims. When God speaks, things happen.

As custodians and ministers of the word of God, the Old Testament prophets did not usually come through as subjects of joy. Exposed as they often were to contradiction and insult, they delivered their message at the peril of their lives. So fraught with danger was their mission, they must have found it hard to enjoy their calling. Yet, so loyal were they to the word of God, they would allow no obstacle to prevent it. Whether God would be listened to they could not determine, but he would be heard.

Everything in its own time and place. So also every word of God. There is a time to speak it, to listen to it, and to be quiet. Zechariah emerged from the sanctuary of the Lord in the Temple unable to speak because of the vision he had within. Before Pilate, Jesus gave no answer. "He was oppressed, and he was afflicted, yet he opened not his mouth; like a lamb that is led to the slaughter, and like a sheep that before its shearers is dumb, so he opened not his mouth" (Isa 53:7). "God spoke of old to our fathers by the prophets; but in these last days he has spoken to us by a Son . . ." (Heb 1:1-2). Jesus spoke not necessarily through speech but more through his silent presence.

In Jesus the Word, wisdom and grace are speechless. In a sense God has no more to say. What more could he say that has not been uttered by Jesus? There remains only the listening to and living by his words. If people are only as good as their words, then, since God himself has spoken to us through his Son, we are only as good as we are attentive to our Lord, the Word of God.

The Israelites were not God's people just because he addressed his word to them in particular. It was the other way around. His word created a people. Through his word Israel was born. God gave his people a name—not a mere label but a personality. A name, as the Hebrew understood the term, situated a person or people in existence. If the ultimate humiliation in those days was to strip a man of his name and place him in a limbo-like existence, then the height of recognition was for God to call someone by name to perform a special task, to share his love. The name Israel constituted an identity as well as a destiny. God promised Abraham, "I will make of you a great nation, and I will bless you and make your name great, so that you will be a blessing" (Gen 12:2).

The Song of Moses describes how God's people enraged him by wandering after household gods. God threatened to take away their name, to reduce them to a faceless people. "They have stirred me to jealousy with what is no god; they have provoked me with their idols. So I will stir them to jealousy with those who are no people . . ." (Deut 32:21).

Nowhere in the New Testament is the word of God addressed to Jesus as it was to the ancient prophets. It would add nothing to the completeness of the Word who is the Lord. There were only the accomplishments of that Word when he spoke or gestured: multiple miracles, hearts touched and turned, sins remitted, power transmitted, signs instituted, and always the proclamation of the Good News. The words of Jesus will echo forever because Jesus is forever. Heaven and earth will pass away first. Why? "The words that I have spoken to you are spirit and life" (John 6:63).

From the moment Jesus rose from the dead there was the ministry of the Word, the one message shared and celebrated, "Jesus is Lord." That message is clear, legible, and audible. There is nothing left to the editors. There is only the remembering and the reliving of the Word. Silenced by some, parroted by others, the Word of God still speaks to those grateful enough to listen. For those in whom his Word has found a comfortable place in their hearts, it becomes the warming coal of God's active and living voice, his burning love.

12

God Sets a Good Table

The basic meaning of the word "eucharist" is a gratitude which finds its release in joyful thanksgiving. The Greek Bible used the word to express human relations. When we offer gratitude to God, thanksgiving takes on the form of prayer. Such grateful sentiments appear in the beginnings of St. Paul's epistles where the apostle blesses and praises God for his wondrous gifts. When remembrances of happy liberating events accompany thanksgiving, then eucharist becomes a living experience. Works join forces with words. Now there are acts of thanksgiving, moments of gratitude. This remembering is not the human practice of recalling, but it is actually reliving the past, the joys of history being caught up in the happy present. The Eucharist has everything to do with grateful and thankful reliving.

When Jesus fed five thousand in the desert by multiplying the loaves and fish, his blessing and thanksgiving were of one cloth. The chalice from which Jesus drank was a bitter cup and a salvation cup. At the Last Supper he did not set in opposition the blessing of the bread and the thanksgiving over the cup. The Eucharist — anticipated, envisaged, and willingly determined from the moment Mary conceived by the Holy Spirit — is one life, sacrifice, thanksgiving. The Eucharist is not Jesus' decision at the end of his life to thank God for all that transpired. It is the whole of Jesus' life, one with every moment lived on earth. It is impossible to think of Jesus from Bethlehem to Calvary without also thinking of thanksgiving, that is, if we think deep enough about the Jesus whom God reveals and not man.

In consecrating the bread and wine into his Body and Blood, Jesus seasons food with eternal value. He adds the ingredient of redemption. As food is necessary for life, just so indispensable is bread and wine changed into the Body and Blood of Christ for growth in spiritual life. The very food God provides for our bodies is our provision for the journey to heaven. The bread that came down from heaven for the Israelites in the desert is now in the Holy Eucharist our sustenance for the homeward pilgrimage. "As the living Father sent me, and I live because of the Father, so he who eats me will live because of me. This is the bread which came down from heaven, not such as the fathers ate and died; he who eats this bread will live for ever" (John 6:57–58). These are the most practical words ever spoken by Jesus.

Jesus prepared to die during the Feast of the Pasch. He readied himself to enlarge its meaning by instituting his own rite, the Paschal rite of the New Testament. With his own Body and Blood, Jesus inaugurated the Holy Eucharist and through this sacrament praised, blessed, and thanked his Father. The Israelites in centuries past praised and thanked God for the manna they received. We Christians now gratefully acknowledge God through Jesus, Victim; Jesus, Victor; Jesus, the Bread of Life; Jesus, our spiritual Viaticum.

Semitic meals were always religious in content. The breaking of the bread took place with words of remembrance and expectation. In our religious experience we focus on the Presence, the meal prepared and ready, the table set, name cards placed, invitations sent throughout the world. The eternal value God gives to food through his Son is of infinite worth to us. Why? First, because this food is God. Second, in sharing the very Person who is the Lamb of God, we might share God's gift with others. Why? Because the Holy Eucharist is God's ultimate gift of love. God feeds us with the best of wheat. There is no better way to taste of the sweetness who is the Lord than to share the table God sets with those who hunger and thirst for him.

We attribute to food a sacred value. Because food is a gift from God, we admonish children never to waste it. When eaten according to a recommended diet, it furthers our health and well-being. We make remarks in charity and with concern at a common meal that would otherwise be unsaid. Grace before and after meals is as ancient as the people who prepared those early meals. Can there really be full and satisfactory celebration apart from eating? Family meals of late suffer as society becomes more mobile. We separate dining rooms from living rooms, yet real living takes place at the dinner table. There we enjoy common ties, holy and happy communion, where God is just a bite away. More than just historical symbols, manna, quail, and water gushing from the rock of Horeb are realities as the Hebrews knew them. Through them man remembers God.

The Holy Eucharist is a rite of food instituted during a real meal. Through Jesus we are able to thank God. Jesus became a Eucharistic reality and not just a symbol as John himself attests, "For my flesh is food indeed, and my blood is drink indeed" (6:55). Have we yet to grasp the reality? Feed on it? Be nourished by it? Become satisfied Christians for it?

Where is the Christ we have lost in our Christianity? Where is the hunger for the Bread of Life we have lost in our gluttonous appetites for the bread of the world? Today we vulgarly define bread as money. Where is the praise, blessing, and gratitude we have lost in our apathetic indifference to God's gift of himself or to our pathetic deference to material things? Where is the personal accommodation we have lost in failing to respond to God's Eucharistic adjustment? Even God cannot share any more than to say, "This is my Body, take and eat."

The Semite always recognized the power of the word, and still does. With deep sobriety, the Jewish father silently pronounced words over the foods of the Passover meal. Solemnly he prayed over the bread and the cup, reliving God's past mercy while rekindling the hope that his people placed in God when he led them out of Egypt. Jesus added to these words his own sovereign authority. The Last Supper became the First Eucharist.

Could Jesus have been more articulate when he instituted the Eucharist? Can we find fault with his choice of words? He certainly does not need anyone to explain his decision to give himself in love. Jesus does need to be immortalized by us mortals. What better way to be alive to his love than to gratefully and joyfully receive the Bread of Life, his Body and Blood?

The words of consecration are more than simply declarative sentences. They are a decree from Jesus. He does not explain or interpret the meaning of bread and wine that becomes his Body and Blood. He transforms them, changes them, replaces their substance with the sacrifice of himself.

During the ministry of Jesus many people cling to him with much hope and trust. In turn Jesus hopes and trusts in them. Through baptism he offers them a share in his priesthood. Through them he desires to be announced and proclaimed until he returns.

For centuries the faithful do proclaim him in the Holy Eucharist. Through him, with him, and in him, they praise and thank God the Father. Celebration and joy is the only acceptable atmosphere for their liturgy. It is in the liturgy that they explain to others what and who it is that God gives them to eat and drink and why they are happy to eat this common meal. Happiness and satisfaction follow their well-prepared meal. When God sets the table and the hungry sit about it, what else results but joy and thanksgiving?

Is there a more serenely stoical beauty than the person who kneels or sits in disciplined adoration before the Eucharistic Presence? The world and its problems shrink at this moment because the Lord magnifies himself within such a soul. What does trouble everywhere matter? Jesus is here! Why get discouraged over illness? Here is salvation! Who cares about the unjust opinions of the dishonest? There is only one decision, God's eternal love on the table of sacrifice, in the tabernacle of repose, in our hearts every time we approach to eat him. We are present to God because he willed to present himself to us. Our presence is our first response to him. All else is a gift from him.

We might now ask: Why does God feed us with himself? He is not indiscriminate food. We do not choose to eat him as we choose from a restaurant menu. He is not just another meal. All God asks is that we hunger for him, believe that only he can satisfy our appetite for happiness. Mary had the answer centuries ago, "He has filled the hungry with good things" (Luke 1:53). God will feed us just because we desire to share him. Faith in God whets our appetite for him.

St. John has told us that what we shall later be has not yet come to light, but when it comes to light, ". . . we shall be like him [God], for we shall see him as he is" (1 John 3:2). Until we see God face to face, it is in the Eucharist that we stay in touch with him, keep company with him, and abide with him as he bides his time with us. In the Eucharist we receive our support, make our promises, persevere in our faith, bolster our hope, embrace our God, confess with joy and gratitude that God loves us with a love that is perfect satisfaction. God sets a good table.

13

With All My Heart

An ancient Hebrew would never have said, "I love you with all my heart." To the Hebrew "heart" meant something like, "My heart loves you with all that I am." When Jesus of Nazareth insisted that we love God and our neighbor with our whole mind, will, and strength, he did not include the heart, since for Jesus, as a Jew, the heart encompassed all of these.

"Heart arrest" is a physical threat for any of us. But it does not begin to probe the surface, in health terms, of what pain could be like in the heart of the Semite. We prefer a minimal meaning for heart pain that is more often than not restricted to our affective life, our emotions, our feelings. Love songs find their harvest here. Greeting cards exploit this to the full. Consequently, when we speak of broken hearts, we are far from the profound meaning David gave to a broken heart when he sang of his own contrite heart. So deep was the wound inflicted by his sin that he literally begged God to create a new heart for him, to give him a new existence. The most havoc was centered for David in the heart. The most happiness was there, too.

The author of the book of Sirach instructs us that God gave to each of us a heart to think with, an understanding heart. Because of his encyclopedic knowledge, Solomon had the reputation of being a man of big heart. In the book of Proverbs, "give me your heart" means "pay attention." Such are some of the Hebraic soundings of the heart, obviously far more penetrating than ours.

The Little Prince by Antoine de Saint-Exupéry is a fable which appeals to our imagination and fancy. It teaches that what is essential and vital in life is often invisible to the eye.

> "The men where you live," said the little prince, "raise five thousand roses in the same garden — they do not find in it what they are looking for.

"And yet what they are looking for could be found in one single rose, or in a little water."

"Yes, that is true," I said.

And the little prince added,

"But the eyes are blind. One must look with the heart. . . ."[1]

The biblical heart is the hub of our existence. With it we enter into conversation with God. When told that his wife Sarah, far advanced in years, was to bear him a son, Abraham laughed within. Judas finalized his decision to betray Jesus after Satan had entered into his heart. When the angel addressed the shepherds, they in turn found the Christ Child and worshiped him with song-filled hearts. Mary treasured all these things in her heart. She personalized them. Her heartbeat and life's breath became the inflection, the accent, the pronouncement of God's every word revealed to the full in the Word made flesh, her Son. Mary is proclamation par excellence. She proclaimed with her heart.

The prophet Isaiah, predicting the destruction of Jerusalem, assailed the blindness and perversity of his contemporaries with blistering words that aroused the fury of Ezekiel. They reverberate in Jesus and burn the ears of those who turn worship of God into routine practice: "And the Lord said, 'Because this people draw near with their mouth and honor me with their lips, while their hearts are far from me, and their fear of me is a commandment of men learned by rote; therefore, behold, I will again do marvelous things with this people . . .'" (29:13-14).

Since the biblical heart is the seat of all morality, the source of every conviction, the guide to all conduct, good and bad, we would do well to take to heart the invitation of Jesus, "Learn from me; for I am gentle and lowly of heart . . ." (Matt 11:29). In the attempt to be honest, sincere, and righteous, there is no substitute for a heart-to-heart sharing with the Sacred Heart of Jesus.

At Mass when the celebrant beseeches God's people to lift up their hearts just moments before Jesus offers the whole of his heart in

---

1. Antoine de Saint Exupéry. *The Little Prince*, trans. Katherine Woods (New York: Harcourt, Brace, and World, 1943) 79.

sacrifice, there is a solemn urgency. The prophets anticipated these words as they rallied Israel to a persevering and prevailing faith. If our faith today is to endure and expand, it must root itself in the human heart as the Semite knew it.

It is within our hearts that we are honest or dishonest with ourselves. From the heart's abundance the mouth speaks, faculties project, actions advertise. It is also from the heart that the lie springs and with it its first cousins, hypocrisy, duplicity, and deceit. Facial expressions, lip talk, eye contact, manual gestures can all be false fronts, deceptive veneer. What we see may not always be what we get.

The Israelites in their more careless and forgetful moments tried to appease God's anger by ritual ceremonies, all purely for show and quite different from what was actually going on in their hearts. It is only within the sanctuary of the heart that we can celebrate any liturgy worthily and with true joy. God asks but one thing when we come to him: our hearts and all their contents.

It could never be in God's heart to abandon us, deserving as we may be of such a fate. "Can a woman forget her sucking child, that she should have no compassion of the son of her womb? Even these may forget, yet I will not forget you" (Isa 49:15). Even? No, more! Especially! "How can I give you up, O Ephraim! How can I hand you over, O Israel!" (Hos 11:8) Yes, how could God, without countering the very nature of his heart? What a demand this places on our hearts! God has only one approach — that is to approach. If any reproach is due it is because we choose to harden our hearts by closing our minds, retarding our wills, and confining our lives with selfishness. But even when we do, God is so kindhearted that he then remembers us the most and accuses us the least.

David's penitential psalm, the *Miserere*, provides a repentant offer that God cannot refuse. Longing for the joy of his innocent youth, David begs God for a new heart that would reclaim the happiness of a steadfast spirit. It is a prayer of petition into which one man has poured the contents of his big heart. Many a salvaged sinner has found confidence and security in this gracious psalm. As long as we fall, which will be until time's end, and as often as we repent, which is always now, Psalm 51 remains available to hearts which search for the proper words of a contrite prayer. As long as we die to our sins, it will live. It is a superb resurrection prayer.

St. Augustine wrote that "our hearts are restless, O Lord, and they will not rest until they rest in thee."[2] At rest in God they shout the loudest, "I love you." From the cross just before he died, Jesus cried out, "My heart loves you." Nothing of a momentary exhibition of love, it includes every beat of that heart from the moment of conception, every restless, sincere attempt by our Lord to demonstrate how truly sick he is and still is with love. "As the Father has loved me, so have I loved you" (John 15:9) still diagnoses perfectly Jesus' lovesickness. In that sense, who needs a healthy heart?

For a good spiritual probing of our hearts, consider the fourth chapter of Deuteronomy, in particular this sentence: "You will find him, if you search after him with all your heart and with all your soul" (4:29). There can be no half measures when seeking to share the fullness of God's love. When we make the all-out effort to adjust ourselves to the heart of God, then the lyrics of David's song become our own, "My heart is steadfast, O God, my heart is steadfast! I will sing and make melody" (Ps 108:2). To our heart's content!

---

2. *Confessions of St. Augustine*, trans. F. J. Sheed (New York: Sheed and Ward) 1:3.

14

Seeking Joy

Beatitude and its equivalents—happiness, joy, peace, and salvation—are words of hope. Since God created the heavens above and the terrain below, we seek after, sacrifice for, never protest against beatitude. It eludes and deludes us, depending on our grasp of the word. So essential to our deepest desires is beatitude that it would be rather strange and remiss if Scripture did not mention something about it, if not everything. It would be puzzling if the Good News did not proclaim it.

Christianity is a happy religion. Jesus taught and lived his mission on earth as a whole-hearted, joyful person. He was "anointed . . . with the oil of gladness . . ." (Heb 1:9). He welcomed the approach of playful children. Michelangelo said, "It is well with me only with a chisel in my hand." With Jesus it was always well. Happy living suited him, was always his delight, because he willed only what was pleasing to his Father. Jesus is God but also a happy man.

We do not simply obtain beatitude, however. Happiness does not just happen. Joy is not a stroke of good fortune nor a gift from lady luck. We find it only after searching. We earn it by learning of it. St. Paul—a zealous and ambitious man, but also an apostle of joy—wrote to the Philippians, "I have learned, in whatever state I am, to be content" (4:11). He traveled extensively as a missionary. Wherever he visited and whatever the circumstances, St. Paul was content and happy. A cursory scanning of his letters reveals a first-hand account of painful situations. What may not be that evident but nevertheless influenced all his experiences was a deep satisfaction and happiness. Having worked at becoming happy in spite of his sufferings, this greatest of missionaries qualified himself to preach peace, joy, and salvation to a bewildered world. He found joy where few dared to look—in the humiliations of Jesus Christ.

St. Paul's awareness of joy encourages us to learn to be content and happy in every situation. This is a disciplinary chore we can master if we become pupils of Jesus, the God-man who never downplayed pain. In fact he promised that in this world we would have much distress. Because he still overcomes this world, he insists that we not be afraid. To link our sufferings with his is to put off sadness. Beatitude then becomes us because we permit it, regardless of the pain. We are happy if we allow Jesus to share our sufferings.

In contrast to the happy Greek gods to whom worshippers looked to fulfill their fondest dreams, the Bible does not linger on the happiness of God. Glory is his primary attribute. Giving glory to God in thanksgiving, glorifying him in all we do can be happy experiences which cannot be contained. We must burst forth with the excitable refrain, "I rejoice in the Lord." And in Mary's Canticle of Joy we find the reason why all generations call her blessed, why tradition nominated her as the cause of our joy, "My soul magnifies the Lord, and my spirit rejoices in God my Savior" (Luke 1:46-47). Here is beatitude at its joyful best. The joy Mary found early in life, the joy she learned through discipline grew, matured, and included that painful experience on Calvary when she became the Mother of Sorrows.

The Old Testament concretely describes beatitude in terms of the woman a man loves, the fruit of labor, eating in good times, wine drunk in moderation, vintage time, and harvest season. The coronation of a king, the return of prisoners, good health, the first-born son: all occasion a ceremonial joy. Loyalty to the covenant, community worship, personal fidelity, the Torah, the memory of the Exodus: all likewise quicken the heart and evoke happiness. In such earthy yet religious experiences, the chosen people rejoice in their God. However, when belief in everlasting happiness becomes more deeply seated, a prudent distrust of the worldly and a purified confidence in Yahweh become the abiding joy. It takes some learning. It happens only with disciplined listening to God. "Blessed is the man whom thou dost chasten, O Lord, and whom thou dost teach out of thy law" (Ps 94:12).

Love is more than mystery. It is joyful mystery. Love without joy abdicates its very meaning. In the same effort that Jesus proved his love, he also authenticated his joy. Jesus generated joy because he enjoyed living and loving by the will of his Father. His one great word in teaching joy was "Father." At the outset of his life on earth, it was the joy of being "in my Father's house" (Luke 2:49). At the end after he ascended Calvary with joy, his happiness was to return joy to its source, "Father, into thy hands I commit my spirit" (Luke 23:46). His happiness was being needed by his Father and by all of God's people and by filling that need. What a joy for him to speak and to hear others say, "Our Father." How many other religions have this built-in beatitude? How many can reduce their teachings to that of happy children, God's little flock, a childlike trust in a God who is to us all what we have come to know any good and generous father to be.

Sugar would sooner be salt and vinegar sweet than for sadness to become a way of life for a committed Christian. When Christians are sad, the primary reason is a faith that has faltered, a hope that has come unhinged, and a love that has failed. The very name of Jesus as Savior is argument enough to contradict the sad Christian. There is only one justifiable sadness and that is sin. Sinners are sad. All the external display of cheerfulness and lively pleasure can never convince one that sinners are truly happy. When sinners sincerely confess their sins, they recapture a joy that is beyond description. For sinners who repent there is a special kind of happiness, the joy of conversion.

"It is finished" (John 19:30). The Greek word *telein*, which John used here, also means "completed." Jesus' death was the completion of a joyful life on earth. This was not a cry of extreme anguish, nor was it the shout of a weary traveler welcoming a joyless journey's end. Neither was it the moan of relief that life's cask of gall had just bottomed out. It was beatitude's climactic moment! It was the closing line of a farewell discourse in which Jesus confided to his disciples, "These things I have spoken to you, that my joy may be in you, and that your joy may be full" (John 15:11). How complete their joy became was historically documented in the early decades of the Church. Thereafter, they adjusted to the adversities of the world, even to joyful martyrdom.

When Jesus said, "I am the way . . ." (John 14:6), he told us that there is only one route through this world to heaven. It is also the way of his cross. He excuses no one from walking this route. Not even Mary, our Blessed Mother. There is a divergence in this route which is more than a wishbone juncture. Will we set out on the road less traveled, laughing and singing in the faith-rooted conviction that nothing can separate us from the joy who is Jesus, the Lord? Or will we take the potholed route of passing pleasure because we want it our way? There are no brilliant road markers, no flashing lights to help us make the choice, only the cross of Jesus, our standard of joy. Jesus still carries that cross in pain but with joy. His cross leaves behind a furrow like the no-passing line on a highway. That solid line means we cannot overtake Jesus in his pain and joy. He is the supreme example of pain and joy. But we can follow with our pain and in our joy. Dare we follow in faith? If we do, in a world where everyone suffers and searches for happiness, it can make all the difference.

15

Passing the Test

The word "test" has two general meanings that complement each other. One has to do with action—the test the miler undergoes in a foot race or when a weight lifter gauges his strength. The other pertains to a person's temperament—the testing that takes place during an illness, a painful separation, or a disappointing failure. The second meaning is the stronger since it is from the testing within that we experience the severest challenge.

"Put to the test" is a phrase frequently used in the Bible. Moses admonished the Israelites not to "put the Lord your God to the test . . ." (Deut 6:16). Jesus quoted the same words in his retort to Satan in the desert where the devil tested him with temptations. In exasperation Peter reprimanded Ananias and his wife Sapphira, "How is it that you have agreed together to tempt the Spirit of the Lord?" (Acts 5:9).

The prophet Jeremiah, a tried and tested man, speaking for God, says, "I the Lord search the mind and try the heart, to give to every man according to his ways, according to the fruit of his doings" (17:10). Since God is the Supreme Being, he alone has the right to test. He is the measure against whom all testing takes place. On the other hand, to test God is outright blasphemy. How bold to test God, as though he might come up short! Yet how often we try!

The purpose of any testing is to discover power hidden beneath appearances. In each of us lies buried potential that we can realize only through testing. Society tests adolescents to see whether or not they have attained adulthood. In some tribal families this is a harrowing ordeal. Without testing, would there be a safe auto, ship, or plane? Those who personally undergo testing may suffer, but it is not trial by affliction or deliberate persecution. Basically, it is still a threshold matter of "let's see," fact finding, soul searching, probing stamina, metering one's ability and capability.

In the Our Father, we address God and ask him to "lead us not into temptation" (Luke 11:4). In Gethsemane, Jesus advised the apostles to pray that they may not "enter into temptation" (Luke 22:46). These are not requests that God excuse us from testing but, rather, anxious pleas that he strengthen us in it. Basic to any testing is the admission that in the struggle for growth, purification of heart, and firmness of will, we need help. To fail this basic test is to neutralize life itself.

Every call by God is a summons to a test. Every prompting of the Holy Spirit, every inspiration, be it from the beauty of nature, the prod of a sensitive conscience, or the appealing life story of Jesus is a test. And never is it without grace. On the contrary, we are able to say, as St. Paul said, "I can do all things in him who strengthens me" (Phil 4:13). We should consider it a privilege that God probes us to test the degree of our love. Because the strength comes from him, he not only asks the questions but supplies the answers. What is expected of us? Passing the supreme test: Trust in him.

May not the humility to ask God for help be the most important preparation for any test? Am I willing to admit my weakness, failure, sins, and submit them to his strength? In time of temptation do I give God a call? Am I so proud that I think I can go it alone? Do I cater to human opinion, social pressure, or just plain stubbornness, and so avoid the embarrassment of asking for help? If so, these are all failures of the first order. When we deny God's help, the testing ends in tragedy.

For those whose help is in the Lord there is never the pitiful cry, "Why me?" but only the request, "Try me, Lord." Pain of mind, heart, and soul must surely be the most intense when the possibility of doing what we could have and should have done is gone forever. Then it will be realized that the testing was a gift from God.

The drama of Israel began on the day its people were freely and mysteriously called by God. Coupled with the choice was the promise that Yahweh would be their God and they forever his people. All that God asked was trust. They agreed. The call constituted Israel as a people of faith, not a perfect faith in the beginning but a faith that would be processed through a series of tests. Israel would be called upon to prove their faith through deeds. That faith must become a historical fact. It did become so for Joseph, Moses, and Joshua, who had before them, as well as behind them, the proven faith of

Abraham. But as a people, Egypt and the desert lay ahead ready to test them.

Egypt and the desert were too much. There God's people failed the test. They doubted his saving help and pleaded that he relieve them of the test. They murmured against the only possible chance of success. Faithful to his covenant, God remained their God and provided further tests and redemptive opportunities. He did not fail them. Testing remained his most liberating gift.

Our Lord Jesus Christ is the generosity of God our Father. He is also the test in our Christian lives. To ignore or reject him is to fail the finals, the ultimate test. The question that all of us must answer is the same question placed before Peter, "Who do you say that I am?" (Luke 9:20). To pass this test each of us must answer from the heart. There can be no crib notes, no running to another for the answer, no postponing the test. The answer we give now determines whether we pass or fail the test.

At Jesus' trial in the courtyard of Pilate, as if giving answer to a multiple-choice test, the crowd with frenzied shouts chose Barabbas in preference to Jesus. They condemned Jesus to crucifixion. All in the crowd had the opportunity to recheck their scores. Only one did as far as we know. That one was a foreigner, a centurion, who upon reexamination and with no little fright after Jesus died admitted, "Truly this was the Son of God!" (Matt 27:54). The answer was late in coming but soon enough to save him. With that correction the eraser came into its own. A perfect adjustment!

The trial of Jesus was central to the test that was an examination of conscience. But it is we who are on trial now and not Jesus. Our consciences now judge our success or failure, innocence or guilt. Now the question is, "Who do we say that we are?" However, take heart. This is the only test where admitting that we have failed is passing the test. If we are honest with our conscience and God, this is one test we cannot fail. It's fail-safe.

Our problem has never been in fielding the question, "Who do you say that I am?" but in embracing the answer. Peter fielded the question very well but soon after failed dismally in accepting the answer, "I do not know him" (Luke 22:57). Peter with heaviness of heart would readjust. In the end he would answer Jesus not with lip-words but with his life on the cross. A perfect score.

A faith without testing is useless; a testing without faith is hopeless. If our greatest need is faith, then faith's most urgent need is a testing. Every testing of the faith is essential and substantial to spiritual growth. Without it faith withers on the vine. As our bodies need food, our lungs air, our hearts blood, so does our faith need testing.

16

God's Desert Path to Paradise

Everything God has created reveals a beauty peculiarly its own. Beauty is relative only insofar as it mirrors God. Shallow is the statement that "beauty is only skin-deep." To be born is already to reflect God's beauty.

A desert has its own beauty. While most of us do not regularly cross deserts, we have acquired a sense of desert life from literature, films, and the news emanating from the oil-rich sheikdoms of the Middle East. Like a swamp, a desert is a seemingly lifeless place, but it has a natural balance of its own. Only a selfish person would dare to tip that balance for the sake of greed or reckless adventure. Incredibly hot during the day, a desert suddenly turns shivering cold at night. Shifting dunes fade toward an infinite horizon. The climate and terrain surround one with suspicion and curiosity. The open desert appears to have no beginning or end.

As the veteran climber dares to scale the steepest mountain, so must the intruder into a desert muster a special courage. To stride boldly into a desert's cemetery silence unprepared to adjust to the environment is to flirt with certain death. Tenacious trees, stark cacti, and hardy bushes stand as grim reminders that survival comes at a cost. However, once we make the adjustment to the environs, we can turn up some startling discoveries.

The return is always to a desert. It was during Israel's exodus in the desert that God called them to himself as his people. From that place without signposts he brought them "out of the land of Egypt, out of the house of bondage" (Exod 20:2). The Israelites believed themselves to be a people chosen by Yahweh. They considered their lives bound by his laws. They lived with the conviction of his guiding and protecting Presence. When God spoke they listened. When God promised they accepted. He would be their faithful God forever, provided they remained loyal to him. If God's promise is beyond any question, Israel had to answer by surviving God's test in the desert, not just by the fierce terrain but by God himself. The terms were God's. At the end of the journey, should they remain faithful, would be another land, one flowing with milk and honey.

A desert is a land which we cannot help thinking God did not bless, wild and barren, where water is literally life; a desert is what it openly pretends to be—empty, desolate, so library-still—we can hear the echoing word distinctly. Israel heard it too. "I will take you for my people, and I will be your God" (Exod 6:7). The word was God's. The almost impossible became possible. More, it became actual.

The word of God was more than description or explanation. It was more than a suggested code of behavior. It was a call to love through active obedience. Never could it be said that Israel became a "people of the Book," the product of the Old Testament. The word of God knows only the present tense. His word speaks (not has been spoken or will be spoken). It transmits life and power. God's word is "I love you" today, now, as you are, wherever you are. God's word is alive in the midst of his people. It is waiting impatiently to share our life. This is why the prophets always introduced or concluded their message with the words, "Thus says the Lord." The word of God overwhelms the power and weakness of people the way the immensity of a desert does. God's word is meaning within mystery, joy within sorrow, faith within doubt, a refreshing pool of cool water within a parched vastness.

Born in a desert, Israel, like any fledgling, experienced the changes expected of infancy and the formative years of adolescence. It is really no surprise that there was the murmuring, the cry of self-pity, the questioning, the compromising. Israel's growth was no different from our own personal growth. Sometimes it called for punishment, the spanking; at other times for reward, the cuddling. Always there was the covenant of mercy. As with the outset of any love pact, there would be setback and success, jubilation and sadness, belief and betrayal. And always there was adventure, always hope—the hope that all must bring when they venture into any desert, always the faith that God demands if we are to meet him on his terms.

We now know that the Essene communities, such as Qumran in the time of Jesus, shunned the city and sought refuge in the desert. Yet John the Baptist, probably of this sect, did not canonize any desert mystique. He preached in the desert the coming of the Messiah, but he also bade his disciples, the baptized, to leave and return to their chores in the villages.

Then Jesus arrived. He desired to relive, not merely recall, Israel's passage through the desert. At the very beginning of his ministry, the Spirit drove Jesus into the desert, where the Tempter tested him. Fully faithful to his Father, he overcame the triple temptation and his success justified his mission. Thus he became the destiny of Israel and the whole world. All testing is now through him, with him and in him. He is our desert, but he is also a partner to our personal exodus to heaven. All ritual, symbol, and mystery receive renewed meaning from Jesus, the Lord. We need not fear the desert for he is always near. He passed his test in 'the desert. He comes with experience. He knows what we need to survive the test. We are confident even though we still fear the desert. We are confident enough in him to answer the question, "Can anything good come out of Nazareth?" (John 1:46) with a "Yes, I can" and "Are you the King of the Jews?" (Matt 27:11) with a "Yes, and mine too."

With the risen Jesus a new time starts for us. God through Jesus is still guiding his people, the Church, through the desert of this world. He is promising to return as the glorified Christ in a final shepherding. Then there will be the most joyful exodus of all to the promised kingdom.

We would be naive to think that an end has come to grumbling and questioning. It still goes on. Not a few are "returning to Egypt," even after the encouraging changes since Vatican Council II. If we want to survive this newest test, we must in faith accept the Council's sixteen documents on God's terms and not man's. Each invites a desert experience, a testing of obedience, a promoting of covenant love.

With the resurrection of Jesus, the desert takes on added beauty and meaning. Where there was survival, we now have salvation. Where there was the question "Yes?", we now have the resolute answer "Amen!" Where there was an over-the-shoulder look for the "good old days" under the pharaohs, we now look ahead with hope to the coming of our Lord, Jesus Christ. Where there was the stiffening of hearts, there can now be a solidifying of faith.

The desert is God's way, his terms. If it is the direct route to a land of milk and honey—heaven, then we should never consider it forbidding or forboding. Rather, as with the Way of the Cross, the way of Jesus, it is the homeward journey, the testing before the succeeding, the pain before the joy, the sacrifice without which the desert will surely claim us. Outside a desert many a delicate flower, a fragile insect, a sun-leathered animal would perish. Without God's terms, the testing, the dying to self, we would all boast in vain of any beauty which could be peculiarly our own.

God speaks to us person-to-person and sometimes with trying words. To refuse to listen by putting him on indefinite hold is to put off that desert experience in which we learn of him the most. Stillness, silent prayer, peaceful reflection, solitude — especially at a time when we have convulsed our inner selves into swirling, blinding dust storms — are not these the call of the desert, the lovable and acceptable meaning of God's terms? This insight renews our outlook on a desert so that we can see it as an oasis. Faith assures us it is no mirage.

17

The Way to Wisdom

The search for wisdom was a quest common to all cultures centuries ago in the Orient. That same endeavor in Western civilization today too often has been restricted to the scientific, the practical, the immediate. Wisdom as a way of living has lost much of its appeal. At a time when we demythologize the three wise men of Bethlehem, for reasons good or not so good, we also demystify that wisdom which postulates them as a worthy supplement to the Christmas story.

The minimal meaning of wisdom is a prudent living that is a guarantee of success in life. This implies a serious reflection on current events around us and an honest listening to our conscience within us. Such wisdom rarely exists apart from religion.

In the sixth century B.C., at the peak of Greek thinking, wisdom developed into a neatly organized philosophy. Philosophy, which originally meant the love or pursuit of wisdom as a prudent way of living, lost most of its initial insight. We took philosophy to mean a study or general outlook on practically everything—a philosophy of life, sports, newscasting, recreation, history, theology, and even war. The mind on its own can possibly attain some very enobling goals, but if they are short of prudent living or contrary to the promptings of our conscience, then wisdom deteriorates into foolishness.

In the Bible the spoken and written word of God assumes the form of wisdom. This does not mean that the revealed thought of God makes us more humanly wise, astute, or clever. Rather, God speaks to us that we might reflect his wisdom in all that we do. Whatever God invites us to do, wisdom underlines his words. Listening to his words, we become more human and humane. Prophesied in the Old Testament, the wisdom of God in the New Testament was baptized with the name of Jesus.

73

A wise person is expert in the art of good living. He weighs the world on the scales of sound judgment and measures its limitations. He manages his pains and joys maturely as they compete for a vantage position within his heart. The wise person does not accumulate knowledge just for the sake of intelligence. Having accepted wisdom as a gift from God, he or she desires to share it with others so that they too may live by moderation, humility, discretion, compassion, concern for justice, and dependence on a Supreme Being. Willing to learn from admitted mistakes, the wise person prudently takes counsel from past experience. Such a person always seeks out the wisdom of others.

Unlike the prophets who were concerned with the fate of God's people, wise persons involve their lives more with the individual. Caught up in the destiny of others, they interest themselves but little with general conduct. They reason that each individual is a towering monument to God's wisdom. Each one wears the cloak of grandeur. They appreciate in the individual solitude, anguish, the futility of selfishness, the inevitability of death, all the wasted effort expended for any pleasure that does not end in joy. Before God they are uneasy, reserved, most questioning. God is a problem, but one that spurs them toward a solution. They know that "godliness is more powerful than anything" (Wis 10:12) and that by accepting the gift of wisdom their lives become "friendship with God" (Wis 7:14).

The champions of wisdom in the Old Testament personified this virtue so as to make exchange with her the more intimate and personal. Now a mother, then a bride; there a hospitable hostess, there a sought-after spouse. In Jesus wisdom walked this earth. In Jesus wisdom accounted to his Father for every word and deed. Wherever Jesus traveled, he went about doing good, thanks to wisdom. A part of Jesus, this wisdom awaits each of us who would be prudent enough to let the Holy Spirit draw us to him. Docility to the Holy Spirit signals the beginning of wisdom.

The avenue to wisdom is a one-way street. Only one way leads to wisdom. She "is easily discerned by those who love her, and is found by those who seek her" (Wis 6:12). Jesus said, "Seek, and you will find; knock, and it will be opened for you" (Matt 7:7-8). Wisdom is the seeking and not the finding. The finding is joy. St. Francis of Assisi offers us the same approach in his Peace Prayer: "It is in dying that we are born to everlasting life." Through wisdom we freely offer ourselves as contradictory witnesses before worldly inanity. This is also being born to everlasting life.

King Solomon prayed to God for wisdom. With his prayer answered, he became wiser than any man before or after him. None was his equal. Immediately his wisdom underwent a test when two women approached him with a baby, each contesting that the child belonged to her. Solomon's solution, familiar to us, moves us to admire him. Wisdom won out and Solomon's gift from God aroused the people across the land. But alas, the very gift, as so often happens, became the occasion for disgrace. Remember, the wisdom Solomon enjoyed was God's gift and not just a philosophy of life or an insight into things. Perhaps for lack of appreciation for the gift, Solomon adapted himself to the ways of the foolish. To be born a fool and remain so is not as terrible as receiving the gift of wisdom and then losing it.

Beware of the temptation to self-satisfying humanism. Be ever mindful of the God who created all. These are the cries of wisdom. These constitute the core of Jesus' teachings. We can very easily turn the earth into a playground and make our life a holiday for gain. Time and again the prophets blared their warning that such wisdom catered to catastrophe. The collapse of Jerusalem bore out their words. The ruins of Rome underscored them. Even now, firsthand evidence compels us to admit that the warning of the prophets, still in effect for our days, falls on deaf ears. It is not that we will never learn. The problem confronting us deludes us if we think it is one of learning wisdom. The problem is one of asking for it. "Every good endowment and every perfect gift is from above . . ." (Jas 1:17). Wisdom qualifies as a gift of God because it comes from above. To be ours, we must ask for it. Our basic problem is learning to ask.

"While gentle silence enveloped all things, and night in its swift course was now half gone, thy all-powerful word leaped from heaven, from the royal throne, into the midst of the land that was doomed, a stern warrior . . . touched heaven while standing on the earth" (Wis 18:14-16). Who else could reach heaven while still standing on earth but Jesus who as man is also God? Certainly, before he arrived in Bethlehem and died on Calvary ours was a doomed world. He taught us to inject prudence into our living, sound judgment into our thinking, sacrifice into our working, and the whole of us into our loving. He exhorted us in our marketplaces to let him, Wisdom, be the motive in our living.

Jesus is far greater than Solomon ever could be. He is more than the teacher of wisdom. Wisdom is he. We become wise when we accept him and love him. That is why he said, "Learn of me." Learning is knowing, and knowing is experiencing, and experiencing is living — in this instance living in Jesus, abiding in him.

As a boy when Jesus questioned the elders in the Temple, he was growing in wisdom ("and Jesus increased in wisdom and in stature, and in favor with God and man" [Luke 2:47].) Later in the synagogue at Nazareth, his home-town folk said, "Where did this man get this wisdom and these mighty works? Is not this the carpenter's son?" (Matt 13:54-55). Because wisdom perceives only those who seek her and the Pharisees were never good explorers of wisdom, they found Jesus too much or too little for them. Jesus turned away and left them to their foolishness. To a crowd who had assembled around the disciples of John the Baptist and who were sent by him from prison to inquire into his identity, Jesus said, "Yet wisdom is justified by her deeds" (Matt 11:19). At Nazareth in the synagogue it obviously was not the time.

Jesus was familiar with the wise men of the Old Testament. He quoted their proverbs, imitated their parables, and appealed to their rules of good living. He never taught after the manner of the scribes who interpreted regulations. He never disguised the truth that he was God's wisdom in this world. Jesus openly claimed that he was the Messiah. Small wonder it all appeared so foolish! It still does. Wisdom does not come cheaply. The lesson is not easy to learn, nor the gift easy to ask for.

With these words, "Come to me . . ." (Matt 11:28), Jesus beckons us to approach him who is more than just one wise man among others. The skeptics demand signs and the proud seek intellectual wisdom, but the humble feed on the wisdom of Jesus. He has since his crucifixion always been the height of folly to the foolish. An obstacle to the Jews and a stumbling block to the Gentiles, the Cross is the power and wisdom of God. Jesus died that never again would his love for us need further proof. God died for us. Let us not blame Jesus that the world still laughs in ridicule at the Cross. Love does have its foolish ways, but never has anyone even suggested a way that is wiser.

Jesus is the Wisdom of every age and place. His words of wisdom reach us through various authors, some unknown to one another, separated by hundreds of miles and beyond contact by many years. Yet all who read their accounts of Jesus come by a wisdom that stirs them to accommodate their personalities and lives to the humble carpenter of Nazareth. Children, adults, and the aged draw strength from the wisdom of Jesus.

The half-wise are still fully foolish. Jesus' words, "Come to me," apply to all of us, all the way, all the time. Our world is afoul because people prefer their own ways to being motivated by God's wisdom.

18

The Cry of the Poor

Classical literature almost forgets the poor, but the Bible does not. There the poor are characteristically described as frugal and meager. They are unfulfilled mendicants, a degraded and afflicted people. Their poverty pertains not only to an economic and social condition but also to their spiritual state. Traditionally poverty was a burning scandal to the Israelites, a misfortune of the first magnitude. They reckoned the acquisition of material wealth as a recompense from God that they deserved in return for keeping faith with him. The man whose "delight is in the law of the Lord . . . is like a tree planted by streams of water, that yields its fruit in its season" (Ps 1:2-3). For those who feared God, there was the guarantee that "wealth and riches are in his house" (Ps 112:3). Theirs was a negotiable God, a bargaining God. Also, the Israelites realized that being poor could be the consequence of laziness.

When the helpless poor suffered injustice at the grasping hands of the greedy, the great prophets always defended them. Amos vented his righteous wrath on Israel herself for exploiting the poor: "They sell the righteous for silver, and the needy for a pair of shoes" (2:6). Micah railed over land-grabbing: "They covet fields, and seize them; and houses, and take them away" (2:2). Jeremiah berated the enslavement of the little ones and praised God because "he has delivered the life of the needy from the hand of evildoers" (20:13). Isaiah thundered that the expected Messiah would come to avenge the rights of the oppressed: "The meek shall obtain fresh joy in the Lord, and the poor among men shall exult in the Holy One of Israel" (29:19). The book of Deuteronomy cites prescriptions that could help the impoverished. Among the Jews giving alms was always essential to true piety and biblical charity.

Throughout the psalms the refrain is the "cry of the poor." The pleas of the poor and the prayer of the persecuted are as one. To be

an enemy of the poor is to be at enmity with God. So involved is God
with the poor that their distress becomes his duty. The New Testament calls the poor his little flock, his children, and they call him,
"Abba" or Father.

Gradually the poor of Yahweh learned to place their trust in
God. They knew that the search for security in gold, land, chariots,
and horses was a temptation that bedeviled everyone daily. They
were aware that self-serving alliances with influential neighbors had
a deadly appeal. They accepted reversals and failures as reminders
that salvation and protection came from God alone.

The poor man with palms stretched heavenward is the model of
hope in Old Testament spirituality. The consoling Good Shepherd
psalm, so familiar in moments of tragedy, expresses the poor man's
hope, "The Lord is my shepherd, I shall not want" (Ps 23:1). Jesus
personalized that hope and inspired St. Paul to write that power is in
weakness, glory comes through suffering, crucifixion is coronation,
and the poor who lean on God are the heirs to the promised
kingdom. The poor alone understand the cry of Jesus, "My God, my
God, why hast thou forsaken me?" (Matt 27:46). For them it is not a
shout of despair but the prayer of the just who in poverty look to a
provident Father.

It was the poor who headlined the Good News. If a good introduction and a well-planned conclusion are critical to a carefully
prepared speech or homily, so also with the poverty message of Jesus.
His inaugural discourse contained the keynote theme of his mission.
"Blessed are you poor, for yours is the kingdom of God" (Luke 6:20).
When Jesus bade the disciples of the Baptist to return and relate to
John all that they had seen and heard — the blind seeing, the deaf
hearing, the lame walking, the lepers healthy, and the dead again
living — he concluded, "The poor have good news preached to them.
And blessed is he who takes no offense at me" (Luke 7:22-23). Why
then should the offer of happiness to the poor become so begrudging-
ly offensive? Could it be that proud self-esteem keeps the scandalized
from being one of them?

Let's get a little more specific about the poor. Jesus was born
and died in poverty. He claimed but one possession, as would St.
Francis of Assisi, the will of his Father in heaven that he carried out
so generously on earth. Certainly there was much in this world loved
by God to live for, but first there was the will of the Father to die for.

When the poor surrender to the will of God, they come into their own. Theirs is the kingdom.

The Gospels refer to the poor in part as publicans, sinners, tax collectors, prostitutes, always with contempt. The adversaries of Jesus created such labels that identified him with these poor. In those days sinners were not those who broke commandments but those engaged in despised trades which usually led to immorality and dishonesty.

The publicans in particular were outlaws. They were the typical poor. As collectors of revenue they extracted exaggerated profits by taking advantage of public ignorance. Hatred of them extended to their families. They had no civil rights. They could not serve as witnesses in a trial or accept honorary titles. Repentance was most difficult for them since this meant a change from a deeply entrenched way of life. But Jesus' guilt by association with them was exclusively on moral grounds. His actions reflected theirs. The self-righteous considered him a sinner because he had become one of the poor.

On occasion Jesus called his followers "little ones," "the least," or "simple ones." These were the poor who had no education whatsoever when the only education possible within Judaism was religious. It was in defense of the poor that Jesus caustically remarked, "Whoever causes one of these little ones who believe in me to sin, it would be better for him if a great millstone were hung around his neck and he were thrown into the sea" (Mark 9:42). Quite a blast from the teacher who was meek and gentle of heart!

Although the proud rejected, alienated, and judged the little ones as contemptible, these poor had God as their advocate. They looked to Jesus for help. They took some of the sting out of John's sad commentary, "He came to his own home, and his own people received him not" (1:11). They received Jesus, even to the point of pleading with him, "Have mercy on us, Son of David" (Matt 9:27). In the poor Jesus they found the adjustment they needed. Once they befriended him, they would never again be destitute.

The proud received the Good News of Jesus for the poor with an avalanche of self-righteous, pharisaical indignation. They escalated their rejection of the poor all the way from incomprehension to dismay to abuse, to charges of blasphemy, to directives that the disciples part company with Jesus the subversive. After all, did he not defy the popular religious sentiments by threatening to abolish all ethics? They simply could not handle the scandal of the poor, which remains a stumbling block to this day and probably will to the end of time. Jesus did say we would have the poor that long.

True, we give token response to the poor and needy but without understanding who the poor really are. In the same superficial manner with which we often reflect upon Scripture, we give attention to the biblical poor. Yet none of us is so wise that we can afford the luxury of ignoring the Good News message of Jesus to the poor. On the other hand, each of us is so poor that only pride keeps us from asking Jesus to have mercy on us, too. Our problem is not poverty but the lack of it. We need to be poor.

"Lord, if you will, you can make me clean" (Matt 8:2). Where can we find a prayer more beautifully mendicant than this? The answer is guaranteed even before we make the request. It is the poor person's prayer, that person who victimizes himself by his selfishness, that person who is assaulted by the injustice of others, that man or woman who is struggling to emerge from despair by turning his or her palms upward toward God. These are the poor all around us whose poverty goes beyond any vow, the poor who are always with us, the poor for whom Jesus, although he was rich, became poor that he might enrich them by his poverty.

19

Justice and Holiness

Suffering would be absurd, unbearable, and repugnant if we could not put it to good use. The best way to use it is as a proof of love. When suffering is so used, Jesus' words "Blessed are those who are persecuted for righteousness' sake, for theirs is the kingdom of heaven" (Matt 5:10) become clear. "For righteousness' sake" means for the sake of justice, not for any legal reason, not to uphold any law, not to justify ourselves or save face, but for the sake of holiness. Scripture gradually reveals that "for righteousness' sake" means for the love of Jesus Christ, the one set apart, who reveals himself as the Just One. He is the reign of God on earth. Suffering for the sake of his Father, Jesus makes it possible for the "reign of God," himself, to be ours. In Jesus our suffering always ends with joy.

A skillful lawyer argues his case in behalf of justice. A judge dispenses justice by enforcing an ordinance. Although always within the law and in flow with it, scriptural justice has a deeper meaning that is far beyond any law. No impatient reading of the revealed word will ever divulge the meaning of justice as God intends it. To understand this more penetrating meaning of justice, insofar as we are capable, we must recognize that the ways of God are not the ways of the world. His ways may shock, scandalize, surprise, contradict, and confuse, but they are always just. God's way is unique because God is unique.

One biblical theme proposes justice as reward from God in return for obedience to his commandments. Deeds decide the measure of reward or punishment. But the more profound theme shuns any across-the-counter deal with God. The justice that comes through in the Bible is faith in a God who is infinitely merciful. His covenant promise, coupled with his mercy which endures forever, and our faith in that mercy, go infinitely beyond justice as we popularly know it.

The Old Testament extolled judges who were equitable in performing their duties. Praise abounded for kings who insisted on fair practices. Conversely, the voices of the prophets thundered throughout the land, castigating unjust procedures that oppressors decreed upon the poor. More than a violation of regulations and customs, injustice insulted the holiness of a personal God who the prophets expected will in time mete out deserved punishment. The victim of injustice who confidently cried out to God for help is called the just man. To him God always responded with mercy. The day was to come when the poor would not only cry out to him but actually approach him. Jeremiah promised that "behold, the days are coming, says the Lord, when I will raise up for David a righteous Branch, and he shall reign as king and deal wisely, and shall execute justice and righteousness in the land" (23:5). The righteous offspring in the line of David was Jesus. Scripture also called him the Just One.

Nowhere do the Gospels outline any duties that pertain to justice as such. Jesus never talked of himself as a judge, even though he lived in a day when Rome usurped the right to appoint high priests as representatives of the people before God. It was not social and political injustices Jesus contended with but the religious vices of formalism, hypocrisy, and complacency. These were injustices against God whose mercy our Lord came to defend as well as to dispense. In the attempt he suffered persecution for the sake of his Father who sent him. This is why Jesus shunned the role of the reformer and shrugged off the invitation to become a national hero. This was also why he directed most angry words toward the self-righteous, the Pharisees, the separated unholy ones who were subverting the true meaning of justice. It was not as a judge but as the Son of God that Jesus defended the rights of his merciful Father. Jesus was God the Father's personal witness for the defense.

Jesus taught that his mission in the world was not to take away the law but to bring it to completion. For us it means that fidelity to the law is still the order of the day. "To suffer persecution for justice's sake" is a blessed experience only if we suffer within the law. Jesus enlightened the Baptist on this matter at the Jordan River when John, refusing to baptize him, heard Jesus gently answer, "Let it be so now; for thus it is fitting for us to fulfill all righteousness" (Matt 3:15).

The Good News of Jesus precedes all the trust that we could ever place in God by merely observing his commandments. The glad tidings that Jesus makes public is faith in a just and merciful God. He comes to call not the self-righteous but the just who cry out to God for mercy. Jesus does have favorites. He leans towards those who, mindful of their spiritual poverty, approach him and beg for his mercy. He finds it impossible to favor anyone who refuses to come to him.

"My Jesus, mercy!" Few people understand the depth of this prayer. They do not know what they are asking for. They have yet to evaluate the meaning Jesus gives to justice. They assume that the ways of God should be the ways of the world. They would prefer to do their business with God instead of going about his business. Thus "to suffer persecution for justice's sake" is a hollow phrase, bankrupt of meaning, and about as shallow as when we offhandedly say, "For goodness' sake."

"There is no faithfulness or kindness, and no knowledge of God in the land; there is swearing, lying, killing, stealing, and committing adultery; they break all bounds and murder follows murder" (Hos 4:1-2). The conditions for such a pitiful state are as real today as they were in the time of Hosea. We enfeeble faith because we do not live it, do not let it influence our professions, our decisions, our liturgy. We appear to have all the motions going, but with no in-depth response to the mercy of God. We pray, but we do not cry out. We sing, but only half-heartedly. Should persecution come — sickness, disappointment, prejudice — many would not suffer it for justice's sake because God's way has yet to become our way. "For the love of Jesus Christ" is a motive that moves fewer and fewer as our need for the mercy of God grows greater and greater. We need to believe Jesus is the fulfillment of the law. If we still need law to love him, if we still need legislation to prod us into befriending him, if our rubrics predominate over spontaneous song, prayer, and gesture in our liturgy, then when persecution comes we will but add to it in our endless search for some law to liberate us from it.

Only an obedient surrender in faith to God justifies. This forbids defining in any legalistic sense the justice we have been examining. The justice we live is a virtue, a strength, a relationship with God. In return for his love and mercy, all he wants and all he ever asked for is our trust in him, our faith in his word, our confidence in

Jesus. Of course it is not easy. For genuine faith and trust, there must be a testing through persecution. Jesus himself is that test.

Jesus' death and resurrection effect more than a destruction of sin and death. They are a revolution through death. To suffer on earth as Jesus did and to prepare for our death as he teaches us is to join in that revolution. This revolution means rising above the literal expression of Jesus' message of love and ridding ourselves of the legalisms that make boredom of Christian life. It is hard, if not impossible, to do anything exciting or venturesome for the love of Jesus if all we do is just toe the line, meet the letter of the law, or suffer ailments just for the sake of a cold and indifferent law. If Jesus had said, "Unless you follow these rules and regulations," the word "unless" would no more challenge us than if he had insisted, "Unless you stand you cannot walk." But when he says "unless," be on the alert, get ready, stand by; what follows is a matter of life or death, courage or cowardice, happiness now or continued sadness. Jesus confronts us with a radical choice. He never excludes himself. Jesus advances the simple truth that if you do not accept and love me, who else can make the promises I do; who else could do what I have done; who else could fulfill the law by loving you as I do now?

St. Paul took the "unless" of Jesus as his cue and formulated it after a conditional: "If you confess with your lips that Jesus is Lord and believe in your heart that God raised him from the dead, you will be saved. For man believes with his heart and so is justified, and he confesses with his lips and so is saved" (Rom 10:9-10).

In a sense our hearts are ignorant of any letter or law. That is left for the mind to grapple with. Our hearts have to do with life, our whole existence, the way we live and love. We cannot love a law with all our hearts. Love is only for God or for people. Unless we put our whole heart into responding to the persecutions that befall us, unless we channel our ambitions toward Jesus, for justice's sake, for the love of him, we will continue to quibble, squabble, and babble about the letter and the law to our heart's discontent. Our lips will have nothing to confess or praise, our faith will have yet to believe in someone, our healing will be diagnosed as a sickness. Jesus came not to justify the letter and the law but to fulfill it by inviting us to pray as he did, to suffer persecution for his sake, to take all laws and to share their deepest meaning with him.

20

Mary: Mystery within Majesty

God guaranteed Mary a place second to none within Christian tradition. She is his favored daughter. The first and last word concerning the dignity, purity, and beauty of Mary belong to God. Her biblical presence speaks softer than her words and certainly much louder than what people say about her. Her title Mother of God designates a uniqueness beyond describing. Whatever praise, honor, and song we direct toward Mary, we do it best when we let our fainthearted trust receive its inspiration from her faultless faith.

The gospel writers concentrated their attention on Jesus. St. Luke's account of the homely circumstances surrounding the birth of her son enlivens our imagination and enkindles our hearts. St. John bracketed the public life of Jesus between two Marian events, Cana and Calvary. At Cana she displayed exemplary concern, on Calvary immeasurable patience. Both were necessary if Mary was to be the model mother and we her admiring children.

The name Mary is a grand old name that was common to her time. It means something like "Princess" or "Lady." Mary was not the ordinary Jewish maiden that homilists sometimes portray her. Gabriel's salutation, "Rejoice, O highly favored daughter" (Luke 1:28) [New American Bible] has a regal ring. It means that the angel greeted Mary as the recipient of God's sanctifying power. Mary personified the people of God. As the motive of God's special love, she awaited with dignified composure the arrival of the Savior of the world. In her *Magnificat* she sang a sentiment that was deeper and broader than personal thanksgiving. Mary melodied in her hymn what all of us are now invited to sing in chorus, God's love for the humble and the poor. The Song of Hannah inspired Mary, and she instructs us by her words. The humble and the poor have a favorite in Mary.

Contemporary with Mary, a sect known as the Essenes observed lifelong continence. Accustomed more to the law than the spirit, their purpose, however noble, was legal. Mary's continence differed from that of the Essenes. A personal God had chosen her to be his mother. St. Luke lingers longer than the other evangelists on the chastity of the Blessed Virgin. He reports Mary's marriage with Joseph and spells out the genealogy of Jesus as the Son of David. Such marriages between the espoused at that time took place before the bride entered the husband's house. Consider the parable of the ten virgins. The finale of the wedding celebration came when the bridegroom escorted his bride from her home, and the bridal pair entered his parents' house.

"How can this be since I do not know man?" (Luke 1:34 [NAB]). Who would say this except one who does not know man? To know man in the scriptural tradition meant a conjugal relation. As strong as was Mary's denial of knowing man, her answer to Gabriel was positive: "Let it be done to me as you say" (Luke 1:38 [NAB]). Eternally begotten of the Father, born of the Virgin Mary, by the power of the Holy Spirit, God became flesh in the person of Jesus Christ. This was history's most important event. St. Augustine thought that Mary really meant that she did not want to know man, in which case Mary would have preserved her virginity regardless of the angel's visit. But the angel did appear and spoke. Mary answered, became the Mother of God, yet remained a virgin. God presented us with another mystery to which our faith happily adjusts.

Mary's decision to become the Mother of God was not expedient. She listened and responded to a call no less real than the calls to Abraham, Jeremiah, Moses, and Ezekiel. Mary nevertheless obeyed, surrendered, and entrusted her whole life to all that God wills. She never did fully comprehend the mystery. But given the majesty of God, why even try? The majesty of God is the first truth and its mystery a gradual and perpetual revelation of it.

Many of the gospel passages allude to Mary simply as the mother of Jesus — as we would speak of any mother. Is there a phrase that could possibly communicate more? Mary remains the Mother of God. Only our lack of appreciation for the mystery of Mary diminishes God's majesty. In Mary we have the motivation we need to realize God's will. We too are a joyful mystery within God's glory.

As with all good mothers, Mary reared and educated her son as he matured in wisdom, grace, and age. How happy must have been the atmosphere in her home as she contentedly shared this responsibility with Joseph. The productive sounds of carpentry, the cool and refreshing evenings after a sun-drenched day, the give-and-take of neighborly chats, and the moments of prayer and reflection on Scripture mark her vocation differently from how our bias perhaps envisions it. Mother of God also means the mother of a baby, an inquisitive boy, a determined young man.

No vocation puts such a demand and stress on sharing as does motherhood. Mary calmly and cautiously aligned her life to the will of God. He in turn, as Jesus, accommodated himself to her. Mothers need the sharing their families provide. When on an anxious day Jesus said to Mary, "Did you not know that I must be in my Father's house?" (Luke 2:49), she felt the pain of many separations and adjustments. Jesus' words were less those of a son than one who had first to live by his Father's will. She heard "woman" spoken with solemnity but never without reverence, underscoring the authority with which Jesus advanced the reign of God on earth and the honor of his mother.

Fidelity to God is one of the prettier blossoms in the bouquet that is our Blessed Mother. Problems pertinent to any faith in God were more critically hers. Her selfless decisions were unlike any others. As God's personal choice, Mary was unique in everything that she did. The decisions of any mother are critical for the welfare of her children and family. But if that mother is the Mother of God, how seriously should we study her every word and act. Mary needed the fullness of grace to respond to God with the fullest of trust. On Calvary she confirmed her faith with a silent finality that was as real and conclusive as the death of her son. Jesus in his dying words, "Behold, your mother" (John 19:27), implied an explicit lesson that in Mary is the fullness of faith. Many went down from Calvary grieving with Mary, but she descended also with head held high. She would be mother to Jesus beyond death — and to us, the mother of faith.

The object of Mary's faith was her own flesh and blood, Jesus, the Son of God. She willingly fulfilled the prophecies of the Old Testament that announced the coming of the Messiah, the Savior, the Suffering Servant. In the Temple, Simeon refreshed her memory. Jesus was, to be sure, the light of the Gentiles, but also he was a sign of contradiction as was Mary. Favored by majesty, Mary nonetheless faced mystery faithfully, both in joy and in sorrow.

In her *Magnificat*, Mary sang of a new event, of a rebirth, of a never-before presence. Is there anything more fresh, more new, than the Virgin herself, immaculately conceived, the instrument of virgin birth, chastity personified? Anything more new, but never just novel, than the mystery of Mary within the majesty of God's love? Anything more new than our faith when it is a daily "Let it be done to me" trust? With renewed confidence we thank you, Mary, Mother of God, our mystery, our mother, God's majesty!

21

Suffering, Our Finest Hour

A riddle. When is bad good, wrong right, and despair hope? When there is faith, where there is love — not a neutralized faith or immobilized love that some research and others preach about, but a faith in and love for another. Jesus is the answer to the riddle. St. Paul unraveled the riddle when he wrote, "For the sake of Christ, then, I am content with weaknesses, insults, hardships, persecutions, and calamities; for when I am weak, then I am strong" (2 Cor 12:10). With Jesus nothing is so thoroughly disjointed that it is totally bad, wrong, or hopeless. Even sin can be the occasion for his mercy. With him anything that is bad can be turned into good.

Of itself suffering is an evil we should work to eliminate. It can be to our advantage because suffering is a mystery entwined with another mystery, our free will. We are free to convert all our pains and ills into useful and fruitful experiences. Let us consider how.

God in his goodness cannot create suffering outright. How outrageous even to think of him saying, "Let there be suffering." Suffering can never, nor should it ever, be called a gift. It can never be included alongside everything else that God created as good, true, and beautiful. Suffering is the consequence of the gift called free will, which we are free to use badly as Adam and Eve did. Such misuse of free will is sin — the deliberate refusal to choose him and all that is good, true, and beautiful in order to be happy and enjoy his gifts. It is this misuse that brought suffering into this world and into our lives.

Jesus took the suffering caused by sin and made it the occasion for love. Instead of the insanity that some would connect with suffering, we can have the opportunity to exercise the virtues of faith, perseverance, long-suffering, patience. Of his own suffering Jesus said to encourage us, "Was it not necessary that the Christ should suffer these things and enter into his glory?" (Luke 24:26) To die out of love for another may be the best of all loving, but certainly included in that sacrificial act is the suffering that goes before it and with it. Consider the example of Maximilian Kolbe, the Franciscan who willingly died in place of a fellow prisoner in a concentration camp because of a loving sympathy for that man's family.

With homespun logic the Scriptures reason that just as we respect and reverence our fathers for disciplining us, so must we cheerfully continue to obey our Father in heaven in the suffering that tempers us. Such discipline goes a long way to heal the whole person. Moments lived in pain can produce our finest effort. We would never know just how much we could love God and others except through suffering.

Please understand that we do not extol suffering to the extreme as though in itself it were our ticket to heaven. Remember that the sentiments of sorrow in Scripture compassionately focus on the victim of pain. They never compromised the evil of suffering. The lamentations we read there express the cries of the poor. They are the bewailings, not so much of a people shuddering before unrelenting rulers, or the plaintive reproaches of the prophets in the face of injustice, as they are the groans of the helpless before God. The God of mercy not only hears these cries but does something about them. He comes to us in person as the Just One to lend satisfaction to pain, to transform curses into cures, to teach us how to freely choose joy especially when we suffer. St. Paul admitted that "with all our afflictions, I am overjoyed" (2 Cor 7:4).

In the Old Testament wisdom and good health are acknowledged as twin blessings from God. Nowhere within these sacred pages is suffering the reason for rejoicing or reveling. Since no life on earth escapes suffering, something had to be done about it. It was done. Jesus entered into the human experience in every way. He became like us in all things, excluding sin — the cause of it all. He suffered and died for us, but not before he asked, "Do this in remembrance of me" (Luke 22:19). Love me as I love you. Suffer with me as I weep with you. Share my experience. In your need to be cured, healed, restored, and renewed, I commend to you the meaning of my name, Jesus, which says it all. Only in it will you find salvation, health for the whole self.

Scripture has never resorted to any Manichaen resolution for the mystery of suffering. Manichaeus taught that light and goodness personified as God are in eternal conflict with chaos and evil, also personified as God. The Bible would have none of it. Nearly all the prophets repeatedly proclaimed one God, a God familiar with our sorrow, an enemy to grief and suffering, vanquisher of evil forever on Calvary. There Jesus suffered and died for love of us and gave proof that lovesickness can never be cured. The more lovesick anyone is the less need there is for a cure. The only cure for lovesickness is loving all the more.

Although suffering springs from the misuse of free will, it is not the inevitable result of sin. Jesus settled this problem once and for all when he answered his disciples' question about the man born blind. It was not his sin nor his parents, said Jesus, "but that the works of God might be made manifest in him" (John 9:3). Suffering as caused by sin contradicts the Cross. Then good would literally be bad or the bad good — an impossibility.

John 17 contains the intimate prayer of Jesus to his Father in behalf of the disciples who stood by him and all those who believe in him. Its beginning reflects back to Jesus' earlier consolation that "in me you may have peace. In the world you have tribulation; but be of good cheer, I have overcome the world" (John 16:33). Whatever the degree of our suffering, if we continue to love, God will supply the peace.

Even as Jesus prayed, he knew he was in deep trouble. The cross was just hours away. Much suffering awaited him. During the night he would be betrayed and forsaken. With the dawn, corrupt officials would put their insidious scheme into play. Meanwhile, Jesus would pray as he was accustomed to pray, "Father, the hour has come . . ." (John 17:1). It was not a desperate ploy for a way out but a turning to the Father when all else had failed — with words measured, mind composed, heart at ease. There would be no frantic adjustment. His prayer was enough. His hour had come and he was prepared to live to the full every moment of it. Jesus had his spiritual reserve. In the end the will of the Father would be gratefully accomplished as it was so graciously accepted in the beginning by Mary, his Mother.

It seems to be the nature of trouble to happen when it is most unexpected and unwelcome. Trouble has many points of entry: the courier at the door, a casual letter, a routine visit to a doctor. All of a sudden the hour has come with no time to prepare, to learn to pray, to build a resilient faith. Prudent is that person who adjusts to that hour by accommodating to it now. To anticipate it is not to worry over it. It takes time to take courage. That time is today, without delay.

Although a more cruel death than his is hardly conceivable, Jesus was aware of the possibility that came with it because he prayed to his Father, "I glorified thee on earth, having accomplished the work which thou gavest me to do . . ." (John 17:4). It was not finished until Jesus said with his last breath, "It is finished" (John 19:30). In the same breath he gave purpose to pain, glory to the Cross, and hope to the hapless cause. Jesus died on his cross that we might learn to live with ours.

Jesus' prayer in his finest hour was not for himself but for his disciples. His loyalty to them kept him from indulging in any self-pity. It would be a time of special stewardship, the Suffering Servant ministering to his own. They would need the courage more than he. They too had hopes, dreams, expectations because of him. The same glory that the Father would shower on him he desired to shine through them.

A Baptist minister once accidentally shot to death his hunting companion. For days he brooded over the mishap. Then he came across a cynical editorial concerning the accident. The line "Now we will see if the minister's faith really works" restored him to health. Such is the way of unexpected grace. In our hour of trial others may not be so unkind as to write or speak such words for us. However, they will think them—"I wonder how she will handle it." "We will just have to wait and see how he stands up under it." "Poor people, how will they ever manage?"

Faith will not work in our hour of suffering if we have not learned to pray as Jesus did when in trouble, if we do not look beyond the suffering, if loyalty to others, especially our own, is wanting. Faith itself will be in trouble. Suffering will be wasted. Faith does not mean we have all the packaged answers to our suffering. Faith does mean we are not afraid of the questions nor do we lack the courage to ask them of ourselves or let others ask them. When that faith is in Jesus, a faith lived to the full and to the finish, then in our hour we will have the answer to the riddle of suffering and the mystery of love. It will be our finest hour.

22

Deciding On Happiness

Despite all the attempts at personal ministration, care, and open-ended love, many people just do not want to be happy, cheerful, or content. The moment that Adam decided to displace God who is infinite joy Adam became the model of all that is unhappy. He became a crabby and grouchy man. Happiness was his goal, unhappiness his harvest. Like Adam, we either choose to become happy, despite our sins, or we prefer to remain sad and adamant to any attempt from others to make us happy.

When we turn to God, so swiftly does God respond that he can never be clocked. Not for a single second is any human being without God's assistance. No sooner did Adam disobey than God offered his help. When Adam saw ashamedly that he was naked, right on the spot God became his personal tailor and fitted him with a covering garment. When the Israelites hungered for food, God managed the first soup kitchen and served manna in the desert. When they needed a guide, God provided the leaders to bring them to the land of promise.

Time and again God offers his help whenever and wherever the need. His invitation is about as simple and direct as language will permit. "Can I be of any help?" Is there anything that God has not thought of for our well-being? The thought is not enough? Then how about his thinking voiced and fleshed in Jesus? Still not enough? If not, we have another case of just not wanting to be happy, to be of good cheer, to become the joyful person God created us to be. "What more was there to do for my vineyard, that I have not done in it?" (Isa 5:4). And again with clear persistence, "Can a woman forget her sucking child, that she should have no compassion on the son of her womb? Even these may forget, yet I will not forget you" (Isa 49:15). Not to forget for God means to remember especially those stubborn times when for some reason we just do not want to be happy.

Satan is a most accommodating partner to every sin. Ever eager and ready to team up against God, he fails or succeeds in us. With him it's either joy or sadness, winner take all or go for broke. Knowing full well that he can be the occasion for victory and joy, Satan prowls relentlessly in quest of public relations directors. He finds them in the disconsolate victim who guarantees him popularity and applause. Audaciously he struts across our stages in the full blaze of the footlights. Under the pretext of legitimate pleasure, he is reflected off the silver screen whether in a theater or a living room. Far into the night he preys on the darkened mind and weakened will, deluding those who just do not want to be happy into trusting that in him they have the best of a contented world.

On that day when all were happy and nobody was crabby, God in justice and fairness asked Adam and Eve to obey a command that was indeed serious, quite plain, and most reasonable. In fact, it was the only kind of command that God could give, motivated by love and the desire for their happiness. What should have been a joyful response just for being asked was not. What should have been sheer delight in the reply spiraled down into abjection. Adam and Eve became both the seed and sower of downright discontent. In them the crabgrass of sin found fertile soil.

The real cause of their sin was deeper than the tapered root. Their disobedience was actually the effect of a proud dare to be as gods knowing good and evil. There would be no way but theirs, no playing ball with God. Managers or nothing! Masters of their own destiny. Servants to none. They who had everything, not the least precious of all, the privilege of serving, became the creative inventors of their own misery. They lost a happy dependence on God and with that their share of his joy. The very meaning of God was distorted, a harmony of life was disturbed, and the cornerstone of obedience upon which a most happy existence could have continued was dislodged.

The results of Adam's refusal to be happy are so disastrous because the perversion is so radical. Every day we arise to ambiguity, double-dealing, deceiving, cheating, hiding, sneaking, running, excusing, even killing—all to our gloom and to the lusty glee of the joyless devil. Nevertheless, the entire story of sin is incomplete unless it also tells the tale of hope and recovered happiness. The two interlace. They do so because God is never beyond rescue distance.

Where there is sadness there is all the more room for joy. Where the devil makes his inroads let there not be discouragement. Unhappiness can be unhinged.

Negatives never stand alone. Absolute negatives do not exist. Every no implies a yes. People who decide not to be happy have a serious problem. The answer must come from within the unhappy person, who needs someone to confide in, someone who cares enough, someone to talk with and listen to, someone who is the solution to the deepest need of all, the desire to be happy. That Someone is God. He was there for Adam and Eve. He is that Someone with us now. As Adam and Eve needed to talk with God and as the Israelites needed to walk with him, we can banish sadness and welcome happiness by responding with an obedient yes. Without God, enduring happiness is an impossible dream and often a regrettable nightmare.

Although perfect happiness in this world is not possible, it is within our reach when we talk and walk with God. We do this by loving, knowing, and serving our Creator to the best of our limited effort. The encouraging truth is that he does not hide from us but helps us to find him. He sent that help in his Son, Jesus, to teach us in person how to be happy. Consequently, the refusal to talk and walk with God is infinitely more emphatic. Sin takes on new dimensions. Discontent becomes the more distressing. The alternate decision to happiness is the free choice to be unhappy.

St. Peter warns us that Satan is like a roaring lion, prowling about ready to pounce on his prey. The roaring suggests that the experience of sin never comes as a surprise. There is always the preparatory awareness. More frequently than not the roar is a tempting whisper, the soft sell that hardens hearts. The prince of sadness tantalizes rather than goads, rationalizes rather than discusses.

This insight was borne out quite well in Caesarea Philippi where Jesus asks his disciples, "Who do men say that the Son of man is?" The answer: "Some say John the Baptist, others say Elijah, and others Jeremiah or one of the prophets." Then Jesus asks the inescapable, "But who do you say that I am?" Peter replies, "You are the Christ, the son of the living God" (Matt 16:13-16). Great! Indeed, perfect! Jesus commends Peter for passing the test. But there is more. When Jesus immediately begins to instruct his disciples that he must go to Jerusalem and there suffer much, look what happens. Peter protests, "God forbid, Lord! This shall never happen to you."

Jesus then rebukes Peter, "Get behind me, Satan! You are a hindrance to me; for you are not on the side of God, but of men" (Matt 16:22-23). Peter trips on a subtle temptation and takes on the sad personality of Satan. The rock crumbles to dust. Having preferred his way to God's, Peter now needs the very power to liberate on earth that Jesus had but a short time before entrusted to him. Peter needs to be happy again. Praise God, he eventually returns to the ways of God and dies a happy man.

The havoc that sin spreads today does not seem to bother us that much. Too often we show and tell everything, except sin, the way it is. We sin out of existence sin itself. Immorality is just the unavoidable thing to do. God is either too good to punish or man is too weak to resist.

In arithmetic addition and multiplication follow different processes. The numbers may be the same, but the answers will not correspond. A similar truth applies to our spiritual life. When we sin we heap up so much unhappiness, but when we love, obey, and withstand temptation, we multiply our joy. In multiplication numbers lose their identity. In addition they do not. When we love we lose ourselves in God or another. When we sin we build up grief. Strictly speaking, sins cannot be multiplied since they would lose their identity. They can only be added, sorrow repeated, sadness compounded. When God commanded Adam, "Be fruitful and multiply" (Gen 1:28), he meant, "I will change you. Lose yourself in me and I will make you happy." The sinner, though lost, never loses himself. He is too absorbed in stacking his selfish deeds. The lover in losing himself finds himself. When he does he multiplies his joy.

St. John informs us that no one has ever seen God. Nevertheless, created after the image of God, we can detect something of him in each other. Being his ikon, as the Eastern Church teaches, we either beautify or distort our likeness of God. We beautify when we love and distort when we sin. When we love we advertise a happy God. When we sin we distort ourselves.

A youngster once asked Salvador Dali, "Mister, is it hard to paint a picture?" "Son," Dali replied, "it's either very easy or impossible." To promote a happy God in our unhappy world we need God's assistance. Without him the task and mission is impossible. When we go to him for help, listen to him, talk with him, walk at his side, the attempt becomes easier, holier, happier. Take it or leave it.

23

Unless We Live the Word

In his discourses Jesus often interjected the word "unless." The average Christian might judge these unless clauses to be either-or threats or you-had-better-or-else warnings, but this is not so. When our Lord said "unless," he meant that such was the case, this was God's way. It is the only way things can be if we would worship him honestly, enjoy life happily, and handle his gifts reverently. Any other meaning of this word would eliminate or bypass the substance of Jesus' teaching. We must be prepared to meet "unless" in Scripture. This word alarms, sends a signal for attentive listening, and hints that following it will be some of the most important truths in the Bible.

Here are three unless statements from the Gospels. To Nicodemus, the Pharisee, Jesus declared, "Truly, truly, I say to you, unless one is born anew, he cannot see the kingdom of God" (John 3:3). This means that only those who are of God, believe in him, see the world as his creation, and acknowledge his son will ever understand what their faith is all about. A solemn assurance usually precedes the "unless," alerting us to the grave words that follow.

Jesus taught his disciples that "unless your righteousness exceeds that of the scribes and Pharisees, you will never enter the kingdom of heaven" (Matt 5:20). Scripture calls the Pharisees the Separated Ones or the self-righteous who considered themselves a privileged class. They excluded everyone who did not fit their image. They upset Jesus so that he felt he could do little if anything for them. Directly opposite them were the poor in the Gospels. The Pharisees were so closed against others that even the Spirit was an outsider. Here "unless" means that if we let God and others into our lives we have the right to enter his life and the kingdom he promises. Or, it is impossible for Jesus to love us if we in turn do not love others. True, he will love us because his love is impartial and does not exclude anyone, but if we are like the Pharisees we will never be able to recognize that love.

Closer to the heart of the gospel message and nearer to his own death, Jesus said, "Unless a grain of wheat falls to the earth and dies, it remains alone; but if it dies, it bears much fruit" (John 12:24). Here's an "unless" that really shakes us. Few look forward to dying. We so distract ourselves as to crowd the very thought of it from our thinking. Many reflect on the spiritual niceties of martyrdom but downplay the genuine pain and punishment of it all. These are inevitables.

What is a happy death? We should only know of a happy life in which death has but a temporary role. We must often die so that we can enjoy life the more. This "unless" of Jesus stands as a sober reminder that growth in our life on earth only happens after there is a dying to ourselves and to the world.

In spring crocuses break through the ground, buds begin to shape the trees, birds build nests. Yet what makes all this possible and alive is death. Blossoms, buds, and birds continue life only because death does not have the last word. Death is a punishment, but it is also a promotion. Death is a reasonable mystery. Death is absurd only if it is absolutely final. Since life comes from death, death promotes life and is indispensable to growth. This painful experience serves God's total plan. Jesus' death has the most salutary purpose of all. God himself died and restored our life. We cannot even imagine the yield from that event. The resurrection is beyond comprehension but not outside our joy. Jesus freely died that he might freely rise from the dead and lend death its ultimate purpose — hope. Only God is exempt from the word "unless" because his death and love are perfectly free. His death proved his love and his love, being free, does not need any "unless."

"Unless" is a most accommodating word. It implies adjusting our lives, our thinking, our believing. Unless we continue to adjust as circumstances invite or conscience commands, life becomes stagnant. Then we soon adjust to the sin of sloth. No risk, no effort, no success, no growth, no victory.

Life is worth living because we believe in Jesus, who came that we may have life and have it more abundantly. He still comes to us in the Eucharist so that we can abide in him and he in us. So, "Unless you eat the flesh of the Son of Man and drink his blood, you have no life in you" (John 6:53).

We either accept Jesus, become friends with him, eat fellowship meals with him in the sacred liturgy, or go our own way hankering for a happiness that will never come. If he fits into our lives, then we walk with him wherever we go. We experience him as we do a pair of shoes, at first tight and stiff; but the longer and farther we walk, the more comfortable is our companionship. We become so alive with him, so in love with his mission, so taken up with proclaiming him to others, we have no time or need to be aware of him — we are him. Sounds beautiful, and it can be beautiful, unless. . . . It is a matter of sharing.

When St. John wrote that the whole world could not contain all that could be written about Jesus, he was not talking about the written word. A biography of Jesus cannot be written. Perhaps this is all for the good, since then we might restrict ourselves to speaking and writing about him rather than living him. St. John meant that Jesus' life has no end. If Jesus continues to live on in us and through us in others, then whoever writes of him must do so until the end of time. Such writing would have to include both Jesus' ministry and ours, which is his. As long as there is a faithful person to embrace all the unless phrases Jesus ever spoke and to live the gravity of the words that follow them, Jesus is alive, still making history. This is why Jesus first called to himself disciples, witnesses, servants, all of whom can be authors, historians, or storytellers.

Are we ready to live these unless utterances? Unless we are, the word is but an empty conjunction. It is like a knot in the middle of a rope holding nothing together. If we take the "unless" seriously and in faith, we will live the words that follow and all the words we speak in prayer, in greeting, consoling, forgiving, loving. The careless use of such phrases as "God bless you" and "Peace to you" is to be decried. To these add "the Body of Christ" and the "Amen" at Mass. When spoken without intensity or sincerity, they become neutral, conventional formulas. They are smoke-screen greetings or salutations, escapist phrases, jargon. They could be replaced by other words, even some that would contradict, without making a jot of difference. They should not betray what perhaps is the greatest scandal in the Christian experience, a half-hearted accommodation to the "unless" words and works of Jesus Christ.

What do the words "the Body of Christ" demand of us? It is that we experience a conviction of faith. Without faith the Body of Christ is just another body. Jesus knew that some would hand him over to crucifixion because they would refuse to believe. They would treat his Body as just another body. Those who believe in him stand by his side to the bitter end. This makes the difference. Jesus reminds us, "No one can come to me unless the Father who sent me draws him" (John 6:44). Faith in Jesus is the Father's drawing power.

When Jesus said "unless," he gave us the initiative to witness his life as Scripture reveals it. So alive are the words of Scripture that unless we live them we will never know God, never enjoy him, never have the courage to live by every "unless" Jesus speaks.

24

St. Joseph: Source-and-Summit Saint

The Dogmatic Constitution on the Church considers our participation in the Eucharistic liturgy as the "source and summit" of our Christian life.[1] Because of God's Presence in the Eucharist, Psalm 23, the Good Shepherd psalm, provides more than rhetoric. Though we walk in the valley of the shadow of death, we do not fear, we do not falter with faintheartedness, we do not want for goodness. Kindness precedes us all the days of our life. The Eucharist is indeed the source and summit of our most deep-seated searchings.

Supernaturally, this all presupposes faith, which is not a source-and-summit gift but a temporal possession that one day will fade before a perpetual enjoyment of God. "We shall see him as he is" (1 John 3:2). Then we shall know him directly as the source and summit of all that exists. As he was in the beginning and is now in the Eucharist, we shall then know him as he is.

There is agitation and argument over the opposition between faith and works. The Hebrew mentality would never have considered the problem. It was too absorbed with the wonderment of God's world. Earthly activity meant cooperative venture with God. Virtue, grace, and theology are ideal notions quite foreign to the Semite, who had no idea of God, only the experience of God. All of creation translated itself into the power, the refreshment, the generosity who is God. Real, personal trust? Yes. But an act of faith in the abstract? Quite meaningless. God was thoroughly source and summit, and the Jews' approach to him was always direct, personal, and at times really insistent — as ours should be to him in the Blessed Sacrament.

If the Eucharist is the source and summit of Christian living, we have in St. Joseph the source and summit of a life lived in fidelity. No

---

1. *Vatican Council II: The Conciliar and Post Conciliar Documents*, ed. Austin Flannery (Collegeville, Minnesota: The Liturgical Press, 1975) 362.

quotable words justify this choice. There are only a few actions. Who needs words when we have deeds?

Words coined by humans can be woefully ambiguous. Except where the Word was made flesh in Jesus, where the Word is truth and life, all other words have limited meaning. Gestures and deeds can also be ambivalent, and painfully so, as when they masquerade as truth while intending evil. In St. Joseph they were the source and summit of all that is right and just.

Jesus made faith the equivalent of salvation. Believing in Jesus is plying our way to heaven. Where faith was lacking, Jesus thought it useless to tarry or teach. Without faith, there could be no source-or-summit message. Without it, Joseph would have been a much harried man, submerged in doubt and suspicion. Mary would have been without her needed guardian and all of us without our source-and-summit saint. St. Joseph agreed to God's terms. The meeting took place in human experience and through God's grace. Joseph was always on call. He was the solution to God's source-and-summit problem, the need for a special spouse for Mary.

God was too personal for Joseph to dispute the distinction between the ideal and real. His thoughts and actions did not permit a pitting of religious devotion against practical living. Life was too human, people too real, and problems too pertinent to ponder such abstractions as spiritual transformation or the state of the soul. God's word was ever active and alive in him. Joseph was not like us, who often listen to the peaceful message of God in our churches but then wrestle with the worries of the world according to another set of ideals.

When God's purpose touches us, can the terms ever be too tough? Once we know the will of God and see his truth revealed, who would challenge the source-and-summit opportunity? Who would not heartily embrace the invitation of Jesus, "He who loves father or mother more than me is not worthy of me; and he who loves son or daughter more than me is not worthy of me; and he who does not take his cross and follow me is not worthy of me. He who finds his life will lose it, and he who loses his life for my sake will find it" (Matt 10:37–39).

"It's a shame!" How frequently we hear this. So often we impute the blame to God. "It's a shame!" Would that shame were not the sham that it is in our guiltless world. Would that the current fare that our TV sets and movie screens present were less shameless. When we calculate sin, immoral conduct, and social evils out of our consciences, then there is no blame. Where there is no blame, there will be no shame. Beating the breast gives way to beating around the bush. The only reputation we then seek is the one that thrives on popular applause.

Here is where our source-and-summit saint stands tall. How delicately he protected Mary's reputation. When was the last time we have indirectly done this? Unwilling to expose Mary and the Child, Joseph, aware of the demands of the Law, decided to divorce her quietly. He did not retreat, steeped in self-pity or self-torture. No, Joseph justified God's choice of him as spouse of the Mother of God and foster father of Jesus. He remained loyal to God and faithful to his spouse. What a pity this example is more history than current event! But when we cancel out sin, what else can we expect? Where reputation before and under God is no longer a sacred trust, then sinful ways become logically consistent.

We must go to Joseph directly since we do not have his words to share. Joseph heeded the angel's summons and received Mary into his home as his spouse. He directs us toward our heavenly home. He instructs us to be servants of the word, by pondering that role, by speaking it less and acting on it more. The nearer he approached Calvary, the fewer were Jesus' words, until there was only the cross to speak for itself. Yes, go to Joseph for advice, encouragement, obedience, and fidelity. Go to Joseph and activate the terms of God that we must meet if we would stop chasing false ideals. Go to Joseph, a wonderfully accommodating man.

A squaw carries her papoose cradled on her back, facing forward, so that the baby, sharing the same vision advantage as the mother, the same point of view, would mature the sooner. The mother in that way provided a summit education for her child. This experience recalls the Good Shepherd parable. When the shepherd found the lost sheep, he placed it, as if it were a stole, on his shoulders. Jesus certainly implies that the lost sheep, the forgiven sinner, then has the same summit vision that he the Good Shepherd has. Having experienced God's mercy, the one rescued could now seek out other lost sheep. Since the shoulders were those of Christ, they were the same shoulders that carried the cross, the source and summit of Jesus' forgiving love.

From where did Joseph receive his vision? Whose shoulders did he stand on? His vantage point came from the giants of truth, those source-and-summit heroes of the Old Testament whose lives were the contemporary expression of God's will. Joseph probed his sources to discover the great servants of God who led him to the summit of fidelity. The shoulders of Joseph now belong to us. There is no adjustment to God's will like the mature accommodation that comes with fidelity.

Go to Joseph? Yes. But first we need to ask Joseph to come to us. Always on call, he will respond.

25

Gratitude: Our First-and-Always Gift

In the beginning was God. In the beginning was also the word of God. God spoke and our world happened. "Let there be light, earth, water, vegetation, man and woman." The story of creation is so familiar—too familiar. The same familiarity that sometimes breeds contempt can also father indifference. God's world that the servants of God in the Old Testament beheld with awe and reverence, we take for granted. Having squandered a legacy of wonder, we thrash about hopelessly in our inability to understand the meaning of God. The root of our sins strikes deepest when we take for granted life in all its forms. To be alive is reason enough to be alive with awe, reverence, and wonder. Where wonder is wanting, so is gratitude.

If our first reaction to God's beautiful creation is wonder, our first response must be gratitude. With all our scientific breakthroughs, our problem is not the lack of information but the lack of appreciation. We have a blind spot in our soul. A visitor to an art gallery once lamented, "I don't see anything wonderful about these old pictures." An attendant answered quietly, "Sir, I must remind you that these pictures are no longer on trial. You are."

God's world is not on trial either. We are. God himself stamped the world with his approval: "God saw everything that he had made, and behold, it was very good" (Gen 1:31). How patiently he waits to hear the psalmist's grateful sentiments updated in our hearts: "I praise thee, for thou art fearful and wonderful. Wonderful are thy works" (Ps 139:14).

"Thank you." Is this just good etiquette pressured by social custom? Or is it just the automatic, conditioned response triggered by the acceptance of a gift? If it is, then we mutilate the first motive that God gives us in this world, gratitude for creating us. Motions without meaning are worse than no motions at all. This is why Jesus said within earshot of Judas at the Last Supper, "Better for that man if he had not been born" (Matt 26:24). To say thanks to God without really meaning it or to say it passively as we often do in the Eucharist (which means thanksgiving) misconstrues the purpose for which God created our hearts. They are restless hearts which will not be at peace until they empty themselves of sincere gratitude and pure thanksgiving.

Gratitude and song imply each other. One gives expression to the other. "Make a joyful noise to the Lord, all the lands! Serve the Lord with gladness. . . . Give thanks to him, bless his name! For the Lord is good; his steadfast love endures for ever . . ." (Ps 100:1-5). Because we have no time for awe and admiration, we reflect little of the happy words in this psalm. Our celebrations come up short of the joyful thanksgiving we owe God. They are anything but wonderful. Our community worship is not always that inspiring to behold.

What is inspiring to behold in prayerful admiration, and what St. John really beheld, was that God became flesh in Jesus Christ. John was one of the best character witnesses for Jesus: "That which was from the beginning, which we have heard, which we have seen with our eyes, which we have looked upon and touched with our hands, concerning the word of life—the life was made manifest, and we saw it, and testify to it, and proclaim to you the eternal life which was with the Father and was made manifest to us" (1 John 1:1-2).

Here John was underscoring his gratitude to Jesus. No one could write this enthusiastically unless he had been moved by joy and thanksgiving. John anticipated on earth the beatific vision Christ promised us all in heaven. The ancient world had its Seven Wonders, but John saw with his own eyes the Messiah whom Isaiah called Wonderful Counselor (9:5). How lavish the Father can be; how grateful we are expected to become. St. Paul reminds us of our negligence: "Ever since the creation of the world his [God's] . . . eternal power and deity, has been clearly perceived . . . . for although they knew God they did not honor him as God or give thanks to him . . ." (Rom 1:20-21). It is sad when the head has all the reasons for gratitude but the heart so little of it.

Concerning gratitude, consider the gospel account of the Pharisee Simon who invited Jesus home to a dinner in his honor. During the meal a woman described only as a sinner suddenly entered. Without introduction, with no attempt at proper conduct, she came to Jesus and wept openly and profusely on his feet. Immediately embarrassed, she quickly removed her head covering, unloosed her hair, and dried Jesus' feet. Only a contemporary would fully appreciate the scandal of this extraordinary incident. It was unacceptable for a woman to unbind her hair publicly in the presence of men, but the woman disregarded this regulation which the Pharisees considered so serious. Jesus gave us the reason: "I tell you, her sins, which are many, are forgiven, for she loved much" (Luke 7:47). The grateful tears that washed Jesus' feet also cleansed her soul. Where you have love you never have it without thanksgiving.

The reason why ingratitude prevails and why thanksgiving for God's gifts finds such rare expression lies in St. Paul's "If I love you the more, am I to be loved the less?" (2 Cor 12:15). Could it possibly be true that God loves us so much — almost too much — that we love him less, even taking him for granted? Might it not be that since God created a bountiful world and showered us with gift upon gift, we have so much that we do not appreciate anything? Are we victims of the law of diminishing returns? We see this reaction when parents glut their children with every conceivable benefit, only to be hated or ignored in return. The more we have to be grateful for, the less gratitude there is.

The solution to this dilemma lies in remembering that before we says thanks for the gift we should thank the giver. We need to personalize our thanksgiving, not so much with select words but with well-chosen deeds. How could we love God less for having loved us too much since his love can only be infinite? Such love is beyond spoiling. We are the spoilers because in our ingratitude we give precedence to the gift over the giver.

We all desperately need to cultivate reverence in order to become grateful. Reverence can turn curiosity into wonder, stargazing into beholding the awesome, the world as man's workbench and laboratory into God's showcase of love. We need to stop and stand still, not only to catch our breath but also to catch a glimpse of God's beautiful handiwork. "Hear this, O Job; stop and consider the wondrous works of God!" (Job 37:14) We need to pay attention to God. When we do so, sharing him and his love will be our joy.